This fast-moving book is load and techniques that you can use immediately to improve your marketing, increase your sales, and boost your personal income. Don't delay. Get it, read it, and begin putting its great ideas to work in your life.

—Brian Tracy
Speaker, Consultant, and Best-Selling Author

Aaron Marcum delivers gold. He wants us entrepreneurs to thrive, and he tells us how with eight simple steps. Read it, and you'll be inspired. Apply it, and you'll flourish in work and life.

—Dr. Kary Oberbrunner
WSJ and *USA Today* Best-Selling author of 13 books
CEO, Igniting Souls

Aaron Marcum's *EntreThrive* is a game-changer for entrepreneurs seeking success as well as a holistic sense of achievement. Drawing from his profound expertise in positive psychology and his rich experience in scaling businesses, Aaron introduces a visionary approach to entrepreneurial well-being. His Eight Laws are a masterclass in balancing the relentless pursuit of business growth with personal fulfillment and happiness and a roadmap to the exponential growth of enterprise value—not just in financial terms, but in the quality of life it cultivates. The book eloquently addresses the challenges entrepreneurs face, such as stress and burnout, and offers actionable strategies for overcoming them.

In this book, Aaron Marcum has crafted a compelling narrative that speaks directly to the entrepreneurial spirit. It encourages us to look beyond traditional measures of success and embrace a more fulfilling, well-rounded entrepreneurial journey. *EntreThrive* is a valuable resource for anyone looking to redefine their entrepreneurial path and achieve a truly rewarding and balanced life.

—Chad Jenkins
CEO, SeedSpark™ and Author of *Just Add A Zero*

EntreThrive delivers a timely, empowering message for all—that taking responsibility for our own well-being is the key to changing the world. With compelling stories and science-backed insights, Aaron Marcum provides entrepreneurs and non-entrepreneurs alike a roadmap to resilience, purpose, and a thriving life. His eight practical EntreThrive Laws teach powerful lessons that are universally applicable, lighting a path out of anxiety, mistrust, and burnout. By first nurturing peace and clarity within, we can rise as renewed; focused leaders equipped to drive meaningful change in business and society at large. *EntreThrive* is an essential playbook for viewing the entrepreneurial spirit as our greatest tool for social good and living the Good Life.

—Margaret Haynes
CEO, Right at Home® Worldwide

Each month over one thousand new business books are published. The majority are about management, leadership, and the financial aspects of running a business. Few focus on how to live the Good Life regardless of the twists and turns life throws you. Fewer still are written by ordinary people doing extraordinary things. *EntreThrive* is that book.

Author Aaron Marcum reflects upon his three decades of being an entrepreneur. He shares his successes but doesn't shine away from his failures and what he has learned about life along the way. Marcum is also a storyteller. Stories about other entrepreneurs, both famous and not-so-famous, make *EntreThrive* all the more real. *EntreThrive* is like having your own professional coach and board of directors all wrapped up in one.

—Margaret H. Greenberg, MAPP, PCC
Veteran Entrepreneur and Co-Author of *The Business of Race: How to Create and Sustain an Antiracist Workplace and Why It's Actually Good for Business* and *Profit from Positive: Proven Leadership Strategies to Boost Productivity and Transform Your Business*

Aaron Marcum is an entrepreneur extraordinaire, a positive psychology leader, and a brilliant visionary who has created *EntreThrive: The Entrepreneur's Eight Laws Accelerating Financial Freedom While Creating The Good Life*. Aaron expertly shares his brilliance, faith, and wisdom, guiding us toward flourishing, and to what Aristotle called, "The Good Life."

EntreThrive is a treasure trove of cutting-edge research, insightful theories, appreciative practices, and uplifting stories that captivate the mind and ignite the spirit. With a harmonious passion that transcends the ordinary, Marcum, an award-winning industry leader, draws from his vast professional experience and enriching family life to redefine the very essence of entrepreneurship at its zenith. He talks the talk and walks the walk, inviting us to join him on a transformative expedition where success is measured in profit margins and in the fulfillment of a life well lived. Prepare to be inspired, motivated, and, above all, empowered to create a better life—one that echoes with the resounding melody of genuine happiness.

—Elaine O'Brien, PHD
Author of *The Power of Play: Optimize Your Joy Potential*

In endorsing this book, I wholeheartedly believe that it is an essential read for entrepreneurs who aspire to lead with character, competence, compassion, and deep connections. *EntreThrive* aligns seamlessly with our vision of nurturing leaders who prioritize enduring principles, ensuring stability and strength in faith, family, and community. This book transcends conventional business literature. It's not just about financial success; it's about crafting a life of meaning, resilience, and joy. The laws, like the Law of EntreClarity and EntreConnections, echo our belief in the power of gratitude, relationships, and continuous flow in all aspects of life.

For any entrepreneur who feels the tug between their business demands and personal fulfillment, *EntreThrive* is more than a book; it's a roadmap to "The Good Life." It empowers readers to redefine success, embrace their agency, and harness their inner strengths to create a harmonious and prosperous life.

—Lee Brower

Founder, Empowered Wealth™ and Author of *The Brower Quadrant*

Aaron Marcum's new book, *EntreThrive: The Entrepreneur's Eight Laws Accelerating Financial Freedom While Creating The Good Life* is an amazing look at some practical ways that entrepreneurs can live a good life. I know these principles work because I have observed Aaron for two decades as a successful entrepreneur starting and selling several businesses, being a great husband and father, and being a faithful leader in his church. If you are an entrepreneur, you will want to devour *EntreThrive*.

—Stephen Tweed

CEO, Leading Home Care

As a health care provider, I understand firsthand that so much of preventive care starts long before disease manifests—it begins with cultivating alignment of mind, body, and purpose. Yet for ambitious entrepreneurs chasing visions, caring for foundational well-being is often sacrificed, resulting in epidemic levels of burnout and health issues over time. In *EntreThrive*, Aaron Marcum skillfully guides readers out of this damaging cycle, blending positive psychology with his own experiences into a holistic roadmap for sustained thriving. Marcum emphasizes the power of community and self-awareness practices that center and ground entrepreneurs, filling their cups so they can pour into mission-driven work. Any founder committed to scalable impact should integrate *EntreThrive*'s wisdom on nourishing interconnectedness and prevention. This book finally gives innovators permission to care for themselves first—a transformative approach for going the distance with humanity intact.

— Dr. Gowri Reddy Rocco, MD, MS
international best-selling author of *Growing Younger*

EntreThrive

The Entrepreneur's Eight Laws to
Accelerate Financial Freedom
While Creating The Good Life

EntreThrive

The Entrepreneur's Eight Laws to
Accelerate Financial Freedom
While Creating The Good Life

AARON MARCUM

ethos
collective

Printed in the United States of America
Published by Ethos Collective™
PO Box 43, Powell, OH 43065
www.ethoscollective.vip

LCCN: 2023911460
Paperback ISBN: 978-1-63680-181-0
Hardcover ISBN: 978-1-63680-182-7
e-book ISBN: 978-1-63680-183-4

Available in paperback, hardcover, e-book, and audiobook.

All Scripture Scriptures marked KJV are taken from the King James Version): King James Version, public domain.

Contents

Dedication 1

Introduction 3

Foreword 7

Preface: Creating Your Good Life Leads to Limitless 9
Freedoms

1. The Law of Entrepreneurial Clarity: EntreClarity 23

2. The Law of Entrepreneurial Creativity: EntreCreate 59

3. The Law of Entrepreneurial Grit: EntreGrit 79

4. The Law of Entrepreneurial Connections: Entre- 95
   Connections

5. The Law of Entrepreneurial Faith: EntreFaith 123

6. The Law of Entrepreneurial Habits: EntreHabits 147

7. The Law of Entrepreneurial Vigor: EntreVigor 169

8. The Law of Entrepreneurial Agency: EntreAgency 193

Conclusion: Traci's Story 215

Notes 223

Acknowledgments   239

About the Author   243

Dedication

To my best friend and loving wife, Heather, who has been the keystone of any success I have had as a father, husband, entrepreneur, son, sibling, and friend.

To my six extraordinary children (Tanner, Brinley, Jantzen, Anna, Elsie, and Quinn) who give me purpose and joy.

To my dedicated parents who taught me to have faith in myself, faith in others, and faith in a God who can make the impossible possible.

To my service-minded parent-in-laws who selflessly give so much of their time and energy to lift those around them.

To my seven loyal siblings who still give me grace and plenty of laughs.

To my exceptional coaches, teachers, mentors, business partners, and loyal friends. Thank you for the countless high-quality connections.

I am blessed and grateful, and I love you all.

Introduction

Dear Fellow Entrepreneurs,

If you are like me, you think about sales and profitability all the time. You are continually looking for ideas to build your business faster, better, and more successfully. You read everything you can, looking for ideas you can use to make more money.

Now, there is a single book that gives you a series of simple, practical, proven methods and techniques you can use immediately to get more and better financial results faster than you might have thought possible,

My friend, author and entrepreneur Aaron Marcum, has written an incredible book, *EntreThrive*, that brings together, in one place, the key principles that enabled him to earn millions of dollars in a variety of different businesses. With these proven principles and strategies, you can save yourself years of hard work getting to the same level of financial success.

For more than forty years, I have taught business and success principles to more than five million people in thousands of seminars in eight-four countries. I've guided millions of Entrepreneurs on their paths to freedom and success. As you read this book, you will find that the practical ideas it contains will help you to achieve greater success faster, especially in these three key areas that I have been teaching entrepreneurs for decades:

Goal Setting and Achievement: I have emphasized the importance of setting clear, specific, written goals and developing plans to achieve them. Each one of the laws in this book will help you develop the dedication and grit necessary to accomplish goals you never thought possible. My favorite question regarding goals is, *"What one great thing would you dare to dream if you knew you could not fail?"* In this book, you learn what *that* is and how to achieve it.

Time Management and Productivity: A key focus of mine has been helping people avoid procrastination and improve their productivity. My best-selling book, *Eat That Frog*, advises tackling the most challenging task first thing in the morning, setting yourself up for a far more productive day. Likewise, Aaron's focus on entrepreneurial habits provides a roadmap to improving your productivity in every aspect of your life.

Personal Responsibility: When I was in my twenties and struggling to progress in life, I felt like a victim, blaming my circumstances on external factors such as the economy and others. My turning point came when I received advice from someone I admired, along the lines of "you are completely responsible for everything you are and for everything you become and achieve."

From then on, my mindset shifted, and I took full responsibility for everything in my life, which has allowed me to achieve my biggest goals, including writing ninety-two bestselling books on business and personal development. Throughout this book, Aaron highlights the importance of personal responsibility as an

entrepreneur and how it not only leads to greater financial freedom but to living your best life!

One of the most important principles I ever discovered is that
success is a learnable skill. *"If you do what other successful people do,
you will eventually get the same results that they get."* I am confident
that, with Aaron Marcum as your guide, this book will teach you
the most important success principles and inspire you to live the
life of your dreams.

Brian Tracy
Speaker, Author, Consultant

Foreword

Y ou're about to meet an amazing entrepreneur who's dealt with the "downs and ups" of building, growing, and selling a business while keeping his family and health intact. Aaron Marcum has been happily married for twenty-seven years, has six amazing kids, and prioritizes his principles and family above anything else.

That's not easy for anyone. He's also had multiple successful exits, which has allowed him significant financial freedom. I'm not saying that to impress you but to impress upon you how hard that is.

Aaron and I met at Strategic Coach®—founded by our business coach, Dan Sullivan—and hit it off immediately. It wasn't long before we started working together, and that's when I witnessed how dedicated he was to reinvent himself for all the right reasons. He's focused on what Dan refers to as the Four Freedoms(™): freedom of time, money, relationships, and purpose.

That leads us to this book and why it's in your hands right now.

EntreThrive represents the culmination of his simple and easy-to-follow principles that will help you, regardless of your entrepreneurial journey. It will help you navigate the "downs and ups" of entrepreneurship with your family, health, and moral compass intact while reaping the benefits of a huge win and a lucrative exit, just like Aaron.

Aaron races road bikes. Winners learn how to "draft"—that's when you ride closely behind a leader to save 33 percent of your energy and at some point, "breakaway" to gain a huge lead over the pack. EntreThrive is an owner's manual for entrepreneurial drafting.

If you ever get to work with Aaron Marcum, DO IT. Beyond this book, Aaron helps founders double their impact and income at Breakaway Speeds. This book can help you get there faster than you thought possible, just like the winner you are meant to be.

—Mike Koenigs
Serial Entrepreneur, Podcaster, and Best-Selling Author of Your
Next Act, Referral Party, and Punch The Elephant

Preface: Creating Your Good Life Leads to Limitless Freedoms

The great stoic, Aristotle, referred to the Good Life as a way to describe the pinnacle of happiness, flourishing, and well-being. One who is living the Good Life is living a life that is complete, guided by reason and virtues. To Aristotle, the Good Life was synonymous with the term eudaimonia, which is when one finds happiness and flourishing over extended periods of time. This happiness is not measured in a moment and includes finding meaning and purpose, irrespective of challenges, setbacks, and uncertainties.

According to the recent book under the same name, *The Good Life*, by Robert Waldinger and Marc Schulz, the Good Life is a complicated life that includes challenges, joy, pain, love, turmoil, achievements, forward leaps, setbacks, and thrills that take our breath away.[1] Yet, through the ups and downs, the Good Life is wrapped in happiness and flourishing. The authors should know as they currently oversee the longest scientific study of happiness ever conducted, the Harvard Study of Adult Development. The fact about this life exists in that there are always uncertainties, challenges, and setbacks. The Good Life is measured over the course of our lives, and therefore, it is not a destination we finally reach.

If the Good Life has no finish line, then how do we achieve it? I would argue it is not an achievement in the traditional sense, but rather, it is something you create for yourself. Only you will know if you're living it or not. This is because the Good Life is not an external measurement of how much money you have, the kind of cars you drive, the house you live in, or the trips you've taken. The Good Life is a mindset. Let me repeat that. *The Good Life is a mindset!* This is why I use the word *create* in the subtitle of this book, instead of *live* the Good Life. *We first must create the Good Life in our own minds, then choose to live it.*

This book is for you, the entrepreneur, to learn how to create and then live the Good Life, regardless of what you face every day in your entrepreneurial journey. My hope is that the Good Life can also be obtained by those who are downtrodden, hopeless, afraid, and struggling to find a level of life satisfaction: the non-entrepreneurs that you influence, your employees, customers, family members, and friends.

For you professionally, my ultimate hope is that your business will experience exponential growth and prosperity, **accelerating your own financial freedom**, because you make the conscious decision to invest in creating the Good Life.

If your happiness feels fleeting due to unhealthy stress, strained relationships, financial challenges, the overwhelming responsibility to provide, and the uncertainties of growing a business, then this book is for you—even if your business is considered successful by the world's standards. Remember, creating the Good Life must incorporate professional and personal thriving. It's about learning how to create a more complete life, irrespective of your circumstances in all areas of life.

The Entrepreneur's Journey Leads Either Toward or Away From the Good Life

This past summer, I was invited by a friend and real estate business partner on an Alaskan fishing trip that has forever changed my perspective about the uncertainties of life. Unlike many Alaskan trips these days, this one did not consist of lodges, hired cooks, and guides to take you to the best fishing holes. Not to knock that kind of Alaskan experience, because I value those and look forward to experiencing that as well. But my Alaska experience consisted of floating on river rafts (the kind you row) for fifty miles along a remote river with the wild Alaskan tundra on both sides of us for seven solid days. My friend had experienced this trip every year for the past twenty-plus years, and the rest of them had at least once. Plus, admittedly, they had more experience with roughing it than I did. I was a fish out of water per se.

Floating a remote river of Alaska naturally created uncertainties, stress, and challenges that required my all-in attention and focus during those seven days. Every day, we would set up and take down camp, battle mosquitoes, prepare our own meals, stay bear-aware, figure out how to stay dry, deal with broken rods, and keep ourselves secure in the rafts as we moved along a river riddled with fallen trees and debris from early flooding a couple weeks prior.

Throughout the experience, I had to change strategies, find different ways of handling unexpected circumstances, and rely on my friends and mentors to keep me safe. Every day, we were exposed to new uncertainties that challenged my will, grit, and creativity. These uncertainties could have been life-threatening without the proper guides (my more experienced friends), tools, resources, preparation, and willingness to figure out how to navigate around them.

I wrote in my journal that week how the uncertainties I was currently experiencing in Alaska were eerily similar to the ones I had and was experiencing as an entrepreneur. Like my Alaska trip, often we go into our entrepreneurship with high expectations and visions of what the entrepreneurial life will look and feel like only to find out that it was a lot harder than we had imagined! Perhaps an understatement, right?

Uncertainties and stress that come from being an entrepreneur can either throw us out of our raft, completely sinking our will to keep going, or they can help make us resilient, more creative, self-determined, and better connected to others. Our entrepreneurial journeys are full of challenges, obstacles, and uncertainties that can potentially take us further away from our deepest desires, purpose, and freedoms we hope to enjoy. These journeys can also take us to some of the greatest vistas, experiences, and opportunities that will forever change us for the better. It all is a matter of how we approach the journey.

My Alaska trip provided me with several parallels to the entrepreneurial experience. To illustrate, here is a quick breakdown of each day of the trip:

- Days 1 & 2: Good weather, decent trout fishing, started on a narrower tributary river making navigation and casting easier, excitement of the new experience, fun moments, embracing some of the challenges of camping, mosquitoes, and discomfort. The newness and excitement of the experience kept me engaged, even when faced with obstacles.

- Days 3 & 4: Intense wind, constant rain, now into the main much wider river making it difficult for me to cast far enough, trees and obstacles, many uncertainties, discouragement, and stress setting in, wondering why I had chosen to be there. Mentally struggling to stay engaged.

- Days 5 & 6: Still dealing with uncertainties with weather but we are finally into salmon fishing and it is a thrilling experience. The rewards of navigating the earlier uncertainties are paying off. Both days were full of laughs, thrills, smiles, and fun; challenges that loomed larger earlier seemed small and insignificant.

- Day 7: Returned home with stories to last a lifetime. Even the challenges became positive memories.

Now relating this Alaskan trip to our entrepreneurial journey:

- Days 1 & 2 represent the early days of an entrepreneurial venture, where the excitement of starting something we have been dreaming about is finally happening. This excitement carries us through early challenges and setbacks.

- At the beginning of day 3, when the wind starts to blow and the rain beats upon us, we have a decision to make. Do we push forward, stay where we are at, or call in the proverbial float plane to pick us up? Do we quit or keep going? This is where grit comes in.

- Days 3 & 4 represent the real challenges that often come between years two-to-five in most entrepreneurial ventures but can come as early as three months. Since my first venture, days 3 & 4 were very difficult and hard to push through. Now, after experiencing the uncertainties and challenges in several ventures since, I still manage to find meaning and joy in those uncertain times because I know what is around the corner, days 5 & 6. However, many ventures fizzle and die in days 3 & 4 because the entrepreneurs fail to surround themselves with the right whos, become burned out, exhausted, fall into the blame game, lead their team with fear, and leave their venture, and their people, broken and discouraged. Their great idea fails to make the desired impact because the entrepreneurs were unable to navigate through the wind and the rain, giving up entirely.

- Getting to days 5 & 6 is tough and kudos to the millions of entrepreneurs who do. These are entrepreneurs who have endured many challenges, anxieties, and late nights to get to this point. In Alaska terms, they are catching a lot of fish now. However, this does not necessarily mean they are thriving. Entrepreneurial success is often defined by society as business success, nice cars, beautiful homes, recognition for accomplishments, and living the life of luxury. I would be a hypocrite if I said these things didn't contribute to my own well-being. I want you to have those comforts of life. However, I have seen many entrepreneurs experience all of those nice material blessings and still come home empty, broken, anxious, and afraid. **Outwardly, they are experiencing days 5 & 6, but inwardly they are stuck in days 3 & 4.**

You see, days 5 & 6 were still full of uncertainties in Alaska. We were floating the same river as earlier, challenged with bad weather and doing our best to stay dry. However, because of our willingness to persevere, we had finally made it beyond decent fishing to epic fishing. We had overcome the necessary obstacles to be able to enjoy what we loved. As a newbie to the experience, I received these days with immense gratitude, even as the rain poured all around me.

To me, the difference between the entrepreneur who makes it to days 5 & 6 and the entrepreneur who thrives in days 5 & 6, comes down to their Good Life mindset and how well they have helped others around them adopt that mindset. They have figured out what it means to create and live the Good Life, irrespective of obstacles, headwinds, and uncertainties. They are flourishing personally and professionally. Doing what they love extends beyond their business. Think on that for a second and ask yourself, are you positively engaged in things you love outside of your business?

As someone who knows what it's like to work so hard you can barely see your family and/or sleep, I want you to know it's possible to thrive.

You don't have to settle for stress and burnout.

You don't have to live with constant anxiety.

You don't have to believe the Lie of the Either/Or.

You can experience the Truth of the Both/And.

The truth of the both/and is when you decide to create the Good Life in your personal *and* professional lives. You *can* have both.

The Dark Side of Entrepreneurship

Unfortunately, entrepreneurs are often glamorized and placed in a sort of hero status, thanks to the Elon Musks, Jeff Bezoses, and Mark Zuckerbergs of the world. If you could see me right now, you would be witnessing the eye roll and shake of the head. Even the successful entrepreneurs know that this glamorization is not reality. There is a dark side to entrepreneurship that can rip us away from creating the Good Life to merely trying to survive.

The dark side manifests itself in a variety of ways. Let me give you a sampling. The unhealthy hustle of entrepreneurship, where work comes first, is celebrated and encouraged by society, ignoring that burnout is often the result of such hustle. Entrepreneurs, for example, are fully invested in their venture, where they feel the full weight and responsibility of making up the slack other team members might leave.[2] This slack frequently requires the entrepreneur to work long hours, well beyond what is normal or helpful for their overall well-being. According to Gallup®, small-business owners (entrepreneurs), work an average of fifty-two hours a week, with only one day off.[3]

Therefore, entrepreneurial burnout can affect individuals in a variety of unique negative ways, physical and psychological. The physiological impact can include severe headaches, sleep disorders, muscle tension, diabetes, flu, and hypertension.[4] In addition, they are at risk of heart disease, ulcers, and many other health challenges.[5] There are psychological impacts as well, including work withdrawal.[6] Entrepreneurs can experience anxiety, depression, sleep disturbance, and lack of focus.[7] Just as important, entrepreneurial burnout can cause founders to be less creative, innovative, productive, and persistent, directly influencing their ability to flourish.[8] Though others may struggle with any of these negative effects, it is compounded for the entrepreneur due to the added responsibilities they have to keep their entrepreneurial venture alive.

These challenges are real, but I am here to tell you that you do not have to be one of these statistics. Research has also shown that entrepreneurs, as a whole, have greater life satisfaction than non-entrepreneurs.[9] I believe that entrepreneurs also have a far greater capacity to create the Good Life for themselves and those they surround themselves with.

Your Guide to Help You Fulfill Your Calling as an Entrepreneur

My goal for you, the entrepreneur, is to help you find a deeper sense of well-being and happiness. One that is lasting and sustainable. In doing so, I am also helping you fulfill your calling as an entrepreneur. What is that calling? According to Peter Diamandis, the well-known entrepreneur, philanthropist, and longevity expert, an entrepreneur is someone who finds a problem and solves it. I believe when you pull back the various layers of an entrepreneur, this is what we are called to do: to solve some of the world's problems, large and small. The world needs your creative mind and ideas.

That leads me to my purpose in writing this book. I want to be one of a few, humbly confident guides to help you create a life worth living, the Good Life, so you can fulfill your calling as an entrepreneur. But why should you listen to me?

Metaphorically speaking, like my friend and mentor in Alaska, I have experienced all six days of the entrepreneurial journey and have come face to face with my greatest fears, uncertainties, financial stressors, suffering relationships, and mental breakdowns. Now going on twenty-one years and counting. During those years, to be perfectly honest, I spent too long in days 3 & 4, trying to row up the river without the proper tools, mindset, people, positive culture, and resources to move through the water faster and with greater ease. Once I did reach days 5 & 6, I have been guilty of relishing in the material blessings they brought while allowing my personal well-being to suffer. Gratefully, I am a quick learner and realized early on that financial wealth was only one of many parts of the equation to living the life I wanted. In 2016, I began to figure out how to truly enjoy days 5 & 6 of my entrepreneurial journey, which has ultimately led me to today and why I am writing this b ook.

In 2020, I successfully exited a company I started in 2008. I had experienced all the ups and downs of entrepreneurship while running this company, which arguably has positively changed the course of an entire industry. Because I had already started my Good Life path in 2016, I had become passionately persistent in learning why some entrepreneurs struggle while others do not.

I have since earned a Master of Applied Positive Psychology (MAPP) degree from the University of Pennsylvania (UPenn), the top program in the world for positive psychology. I felt called to do this in order to truly be in a position to help my fellow entrepreneurs create the life they want. During this transformational program, I studied under many brilliant minds in this field, including the father of positive psychology, Dr. Martin Seligman, who by the way, is one of the most humble, compassionate, and present human beings I have ever had the honor of associating wi th.

In 2011, Seligman introduced PERMA, the five measurable elements of well-being, in his book *Flourish*. PERMA stands for Positive Emotion, Engagement, Relationships, Meaning, and Accomplishment. All are vital elements to well-being. You will find these elements interwoven throughout the eight laws of entrepreneurial thriving because of the influence positive psychology has had on this work.

Though my life is definitely not perfect and even messy at times, I can promise honesty, congruence, and integrity as you read from these pages. I want to be your guide because I have made my own mistakes along my own entrepreneurial journey, giving into burnout, uncertainty, and stress. The best guides are often the ones who have made the biggest mistakes. By those criteria alone, I am more than capable of guiding you as you seek to create the Good Life for you and your loved ones! I have also done the hard work of learning the science of well-being, positive psychology, and how

it can help entrepreneurs live the life they originally dreamed of li
ving.

Along the way, I discovered how to separate myself from my
companies, how to grow a business that can prosper without de-
stroying me in the process, and how to thrive personally as an
entrepreneur.

As your guide, my hope is that by helping you, the entrepreneur,
find personal flourishing and the Good Life, you will positively
impact the lives of those in your family, team members, customers,
and community. Entrepreneurs make the world go round, and if
you are happier and creating your best life, then the world becomes
better because of you.

What to Expect

Each chapter of *EntreThrive* dives deep into one of the eight laws,
providing research that demonstrates why these laws are instrumental to thriving as an entrepreneur. The chapters also teach
you how to implement these laws into your life, beginning with
a "crawl," progressing to a "walk," and finally making it to a "run."
These terms—crawl, walk, and run—are derived from Martin
Luther King, Jr.'s famous quote:

*If you can't fly then run, if you can't run then walk, if you can't
walk then crawl,*

but whatever you do you have to keep moving forward.[10]

No matter where you find yourself in relation to these laws, you
can always begin with a crawl. The goal is to make progress in each
area because that's where EntreThriving will truly happen. Our
final aim is to fly. This is where we embrace each law's plan and

experience growth. By all means, if you're already ready to fly now, go for it! Some will need to take it slow while others will want to 10x their well-being in ninety days. Just be honest about where you are and make room for the necessary steps required on the consistent road of flourishing.

Keep in mind that we are all human, so we're never going to fulfill any of these laws perfectly. At times, you might even drop down to a crawl after experiencing a run. The key is simply having the self-awareness to know where you are so you can get back to where you want to be. I speak from personal experience, as I'm always working on these laws.

If you fail to invest in creating a life worth living, an abundant life that includes building financial wealth alongside peace, happiness, and joy; then can you really call your life abundant and meaningful? Financial wealth is certainly rewarding but empty without having abundance in our relationships, workplace, creations, habits, health, and freedoms. **The fact is your financial freedom is tied directly to each of the laws in this book. These laws are the accelerator principles that will guide you towards greater wealth and prosperity.** The Good Life marries our professional abundance with our personal abundance. You can have both and that, dear friend and entrepreneur, is a life worth living.

Are you ready to flourish?

Are you ready to create the Good Life?

Let's start unpacking each of the eight laws and begin thriving!

This simple graphic demonstrates the impact creating the Good Life, which starts with implementing these eight laws, can have on accelerating your financial freedom:

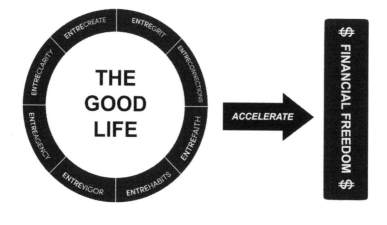

CHAPTER ONE

The Law of Entrepreneurial Clarity: EntreClarity

YOUR GUIDING TRUTHS ILLUMINATE YOUR WAY.

Life is never made unbearable by circumstances, but only by lack of meaning and purpose.
—Viktor Frankl

I was overwhelmed and beyond exhausted. To make matters worse, I'd been sleeping underneath my desk in a last-ditch effort to meet a significant work deadline. Was this really an entrepreneur's reality? Curled up in a sleeping bag on an uncomfortable floor with the weight of the world on their shoulders? I had already built and sold one business, how was I here? Nobody told me the entrepreneur's "starter pack" included permanent dark circles under the eyes, a sleeping bag, and no pillow for a solo office sleepover. Referring back to my Alaska trip, I was on day 3 of my journey, beaten down and bruised a bit.

Halfway through building my first company, a home-care agency, I caught a vision. This industry needed more data analytics. It needed a line of communication from the employees and customers to the people at the top. These changes were vital to the improvement of the industry. After making this realization, I felt giddy. What if this was something I could do? After all, if not me, then who? While I had no background in data analytics, I somehow managed to convince the industry trade association to let me create an industry benchmarking study. Not only would they allow me to do it, they would endorse it as well.

I recognized how valuable the data could be and wanted to use this new tool to publicize my new company's name. So, I spent what seemed like all of my time and energy on this project. It was just me, day after day, week after week, month after month, working on this groundbreaking study.

The excitement and passion I had felt in the beginning could only fuel me for so long. I probably felt similar to my daughter's car when it was months past the due date for an oil change. I was about to break down.

I had worn myself out to a dangerous level. Unfortunately, a fast-approaching publication deadline loomed over my head like an unrelenting storm cloud. I knew if I was going to make the deadline, I couldn't afford more than a few hours of sleep in the upcoming days. So there I was, at the end of my rope, chugging five-hour energy shots for the first time in my life.

Eventually, I reached a breaking point. Sleep begged me to give it some attention, so I crawled under my desk, got into my sleeping bag, and began to bawl. Staring at my office wall, I was lost in a sea of uncertainty, drowning in my overwhelmed thoughts.

What was I thinking when agreeing to do this? Could I really pull this off? Was I lying to myself?

Even if I somehow managed to accomplish it, would it be worth it?

Unsurprisingly, things at home were suffering. I was spending my days and nights in a tight office instead of at home with my family.

It was there, under the desk curled up crying in my sleeping bag, that I reached a turning point. Tears were blurring my vision, but not just physically. The vision for my business was also blurred and muddied. Searching within myself for the passion I had chosen, I remembered my original entrepreneurial vision and what I now call my Guiding Truths. The vision was hanging on my wall to the left of my desk. I knew what this company could do over the next ten years. I knew the impact it would have on an entire industry and for my family. This renewed vision and clarity brought forth a new vitality, something I'd never found at the bottom of one of those energy shots. I immediately got up off of the floor, got back to work, and met the deadline.

Since that pivotal night, all of the vision I had for my company has come true and even more so. The company I started is currently one of the top brands in the home-care space, and I couldn't be prouder.

I discovered through that grueling process that having clarity—a vision of where I was going—is what pushed me to the finish line. Because I knew where I wanted to go, I persevered. I picked my passion and held to it tightly. And this vision didn't apply only to my company, it applied to my life as well. I saw where I wanted to be in life, and I knew the company was the vehicle to get there. Clarity was the much-needed oil change.

This clarity—my under-the-desk vision—allowed me to continue to push forward for several more years and deal with the many challenges and struggles along the way. Clarity is key to the EntreThrive model. Without clarity, you're like a ship lost at sea, but with it, your path becomes illuminated and you can make your way forward, achieving goals in your life you once thought impossible. Most importantly, clarity helps you lean into the struggles while living the Good Life simultaneously!

Problems EntreClarity Solves

Many entrepreneurs struggle with a lack of vision or direction.

They need clarity.

At its core, EntreClarity is when an entrepreneur's vision for themselves and their business is so vividly powerful and exciting, they are willing to push through all the uncertainties, challenges, and obstacles to accomplish it. EntreClarity brings the power to fight the symptoms of stress and burnout. By gaining clarity on our purpose and impact, entrepreneurs can face those significant headwinds that certainly come. We stay on the right path by keeping the bigger picture in mind, never forgetting *where* we are going and *why*.

EntreClarity will keep you moving forward even when the going, inevitably, gets tough.

The Psychological Well-Being Model (PWB), developed by Carol Ryff, the respected psychologist and researcher, comprises six elements of well-being. Though this model was developed in 1989, Ryff and her colleague Nadav Shir took the same elements of this model and applied them to entrepreneurial well-being in

2020. The elements are (1) purpose in life, (2) autonomy, (3) positive relationships, (4) environmental mastery, (5) personal growth, and (6) self-acceptance.[11] Throughout this book, I will tie some of these elements to the laws, starting with the first one, purpose in life. It was this later research, surrounding entrepreneurial well-being, which inspired my thesis for my master's degree. That thesis later led me to develop the EntreThrive eight laws.

According to Ryff and Shir, an entrepreneur's business activities must be in alignment with their purpose and values, as they continually pursue their entrepreneurial goals.[12] This alignment of purpose and business involves incorporating one's moral standards, virtues, and meaning into the impact they want their business to have in the world. Entrepreneurs who lack a purpose or fail to align their business with their purpose might make a lot of sales and find financial success, but still find themselves falling short of living the life they want.

EntreClarity CRAWL: Define Your Guiding Truths

In 2006, four years into my first entrepreneurial venture, I worked with a performance coach to create a personal mission statement, inspired by the likes of Stephen Covey (*The 7 Habits of Highly Effective People*) and Michael Gerber (*The E-Myth Revisited*). Though they use different titles for a personal mission statement, the process of getting to it is similar. Start by asking yourself one defining question: *What do you want people to say about you at your funeral?* This simple exercise forever changed the trajectory of my entrepreneurial journey because it helped me connect back to why

I started my business in the first place and my purpose behind all the sacrifices up to that point.

Since then, my personal mission statement has evolved and has become more of a declaration to myself of what I truly want out of life. It is, however, more than just a declaration. It is what I want to be true about myself at all times. Truths are realities that are immovable. Regardless of negative comments that others might say about me, or the influence of a society that doesn't always have my best interest in mind, my truths stay the same. But only if I live by them! Otherwise, truths are just words.

To hold me accountable to the truths that I am constantly striving to uphold, I have changed my declarations to my *Guiding Truths*. These truths are my lighthouse in a storm, a compass when others try to disorient me, and serve as a GPS to get me to my desired destinations. My Guiding Truths remind me that my business is not my life. Let me say that again: your business is not your life. In fact, our businesses can rob us of experiencing life at its fullest if the business becomes our purpose in life. Our businesses serve our purpose, not the other way around.

A personal Guiding Truth helps keep the focus on the holistic perspective of your life, personally and professionally. However, an important point must be made about your Guiding Truths. It is not a big hairy audacious goal (BHAG, a concept by Jim Collins), a Moonshot (Peter Diamandis), or other important clear goals you want to achieve in your life. Your Guiding Truths simply help you make BHAGs, Moonshots, and big goals align with your why and future self. It is your compass as you create the Good Life for yourself, which must include big goals and Moonshots.

In developing my Guiding Truths, I answered timeless questions that helped me envision what I wanted to be true about my future self. Questions like, "what characteristics do you value most in life," and "what areas of your life create the most meaning for you?" Questions like these go deeper than what you want others to say about you at your funeral. They deal with the past, present, and future wants, hopes, and desires. Your truths.

As an example, I will be vulnerable and share my own Guiding Truths which have remained the same since 2006. They have illuminated my way. I have it posted on a large canvas by my office desk to remind me of my *why*. It was on my wall in 2010, while lying under my desk, which inspired me to not give up on my dream.

My mind is at peace.
My actions reflect character.
My hands provide service.
My body is in good health.
My days are full of laughter.
My family receives my time.
My ventures create freedom.
My life is filled with abundance.
My heart belongs to Christ.

I recently took my Guiding Truths and harnessed the power of AI, which put it in a statement format. Here it is in the newer format: *I strive to embody character in action, serve with my hands, and prioritize my family's well-being. I cherish a life of health, laughter, and abundance, with my heart devoted to Christ.*

To help you find your Guiding Truths, we have created an online tool that will help you think deeper and develop your own. To access this free tool, called our *EntreClarity Guide,* go to Entrethrive.com/Resources.

Referring to my own Guiding Truths, I want you to notice something. It does not mention my business. My business simply is one of my primary vehicles designed to help bring my Guiding Truths to fruition. **These truths, for me personally, are my path to the Good Life** and something I continually strive for. I often fall short in some areas while excelling in others. That is why it is still relevant to me today. I never fully reach 100 percent all at once...therefore, I am constantly working in each area.

Remember in the introduction how I said the Good Life is a mindset? So are my Guiding Truths. I must first create what they look like in my mind, then choose to live them in the way I show up in life, every day.

Guiding Truths Must Spark Positive Emotions

Start building out your Guiding Truths and take the time necessary to create one that elicits positive emotions that are important to you. This is the first "P" in PERMA, Dr. Martin Seligman's five elements of positive psychology and an element that must exist if we are to create the Good Life.

The popular psychologist Barbara Fredrickson, author of *Positivity,* identifies ten positive emotions that each of us attach different meanings and feelings to. They are joy, gratitude, serenity, interest, hope, pride, amusement, inspiration, awe, and love. Through years of research, Fredrickson and her team found that these positive emotions broaden one's awareness of what actions they can take towards their goals and aspirations.[13]

Positive emotions broaden our mindsets. Fredrickson's research then expanded into another powerful concept which focused on how positive emotions build new resources and abilities that help not only with our survival but also our capacity to thrive. Fredrickson combined the broadening of the mindset and the building of new capabilities and resources into one overarching theory entitled the *Broaden and Build Theory*. This theory underpins the importance and impact positive emotions have on our well-being and why they should be incorporated in your Guiding Truths.

By doing so, your mindset should broaden, with actions to follow, while also building new capabilities. Watch for these emotions as you write your Guiding Truths. Which ones do you want to feel the strongest? Circle two-to-three and focus on writing, so those emotions come out in the statement. Have fun with it. Download the *EntreClarity Guide,* which will help you develop your own Guiding Truths, at **EntreThrive.com/Resources.** This guide also includes another powerful tool, *The Breakaway Narrative,* that I will be discussing soon.

To help you find your Guiding Truths, examine nine areas:

1. Purpose: When you look at the people you admire most, what quality or beliefs do they possess? List your top three-to-five.

2. Relationships: In one short sentence, how do you want to be remembered by those you interact with daily?

3. Decision-making: What are your non-negotiables? Those things you are unwilling to compromise on.

4. Contribution: Briefly describe one worthy cause you currently feel passionate about and why.

5. Personal Growth: In the future, how do you want to handle failure and success?

6. Physical health: Five years from now, what do you want to be true about your physical health?

7. Faith: Does faith in God (Transcendent, a higher power) an important guide to your future self? If yes, in a short sentence, describe your desirable relationship with God in the future.

8. Professional impact: In a short sentence, describe how your role at work has a positive impact on your team, communities, and society.

9. Positive emotions: If you had no limitations, what is one thing you would want to accomplish in the next year? List three positive emotions you believe will be a result of that accomplishment.

Once you have a draft, share it with someone who might benefit from a better you. Your spouse, significant other, parent, close friend, etc. Be vulnerable. Allow feedback, but don't change anything if it doesn't speak to you and what you want to become.

Your Guiding Truths can be your compass that guides your choices towards a more flourishing life, personally and professionally.

EntreClarity WALK: Clarity Through Self-Awareness and Self-Acceptance

With your Guiding Truths in hand, you are ready to walk and gain a deeper sense of clarity through self-awareness and self-acceptance. Let's start with self-acceptance, which according to Ryff's PWB model, is when the entrepreneur has a positive evaluation of who they are and what they have become. To accept ourselves means we accept who we are today, knowing we can change. As one writer put it:

"Self-acceptance...means to deeply and totally accept every aspect of yourself unconditionally and without exception."[14]

In order to accept yourself, however, you must understand yourself. In short, self-awareness leads to self-acceptance. The two concepts go hand-in-hand. Self-awareness means we recognize our personal strengths and weaknesses. We honestly evaluate ourselves and acknowledge our challenges and what we bring to our businesses and relationships. Once we have done the hard work of becoming self-aware, we then accept ourselves, just as we are, both the good and the bad. Each plays an important role in creating clarity in our lives.

In addition, the purpose of self-acceptance and self-awareness isn't to belittle ourselves and highlight all of our flaws. Unfortunately, we tend to ruminate on how far we still have to go and all we lack. In our mind, everyone has it more together than we do. However, we want to stay focused on what Dan Sullivan calls "the gains."[15] Here we acknowledge our progress, our accomplishments, and how far we've come, as opposed to obsessing on the gap of where we *want* to be.

By focusing on our various gains, we can live with gratitude, instead of disappointment, because we track and measure our progress against who we used to be. By choosing to notice the gains we've made, our confidence, satisfaction, and happiness grow.[16] This increased confidence allows us to set bigger goals for ourselves and aim for the stars because we realize we do have it within us to change, grow, and achieve.

Self-awareness also means we discover where we would like to go. It's not just about today. It's about tomorrow. Who do I want to be in the future? What do I truly want from my life? Getting to know yourself and your dreams is all a part of self-awareness and self-acceptance.

Why Self-Acceptance Matters

Self-acceptance is fundamental to our overall well-being. Entrepreneurs who accept themselves tend to reveal their authentic selves when they interact with others, especially those deeper relationships.[17] Because they accept who they are, they aren't worried about the judgements and criticisms of others. They feel free to live openly and honestly.

Additionally, self-accepting entrepreneurs are more likely to overcome self-doubt and possess greater confidence, as they understand their limitations don't define them. They have the ability to ward off harsh criticism because they understand they are a work in progress and accept where they are.[18] While accepting their current self, they also know who they are today is not who they will be in the future.

Years ago, I implemented EOS® (Entrepreneurial Operating System®) into my business, and the experience was transformational. During one EOS session, we analyzed the company's leadership team and received feedback on how well we performed on our core values. As the CEO, founder, and visionary for the company, it was pretty disappointing to discover I'd been rated a "plus-minus" on two of the company's core values (in EOS, a plus minus means you sometimes do not behave in this way). My peers believed I fell short on two of my own company's core values, and it hit me hard.

Initially, I probably responded defensively to the negative feedback, but later, I talked with my COO about it and did some self-reflection. I discovered what my team said was true—I didn't listen to new ideas. It was "my way or no way." Even worse, this leadership style spilled into my personal life and affected relationships as well.

The honest feedback helped me become aware of my weaknesses and accept them. Once I accepted them, I could make the necessary changes. I no longer operate with the "my way or no way" mindset. I can't afford to. I'm more open to others' opinions, and this willingness to listen to others and rely on my team has helped me scale my companies. Without the EOS exercise, I would not have been forced to face my weaknesses. Not only that but my leadership style could have stayed the same, stalling growth within myself, the business and those who trusted me enough to work for me.

My self-awareness led to my self-acceptance.

My self-acceptance led to my change.

Self-Awareness through Elimination

Self-awareness isn't merely knowing what you want. It's also knowing what you don't want. As we begin our journey of self-awareness, the first step is to start eliminating those things in your life that do not serve you. Letting go of what doesn't work helps us become who we were meant to be as we create space in our lives for that which moves us towards our bigger dreams.

Entrepreneur, best-selling author, and performance coach Ed Mylett interviewed Academy Award-winning actor Matthew Mc-Conaughey, and the pair discussed finding your identity and discovering what truly feeds you and your soul. According to Mc-Conaughey, finding your identity is more about elimination than a process of discovery.[19] The first step of finding out who you are is finding out who you aren't, which requires self-awareness of what is and isn't important to you as a human being. This is why the exercise of the Guiding Truths is so important. It helps define what is truly important to you.

Pay attention to the habits, people, and places that don't feed you, and begin eliminating those things from your life. By doing so, you inevitably make room for what does feed you.[20] In the process, you discover who you truly are and what matters to you. Mihaly Csikszentmihalyi, also known as the Father of Flow, put it this way: start doing more of what you love and less of what you hate.[21]

Status-Seeking Is not Thriving

Entrepreneurs want to make a big impact. However, part of our self-acceptance and self-awareness means we must dig deep and ask ourselves what our motivation is for wanting or striving towards something. We do this not so we can explain or justify our wanting to others, but to internally check our intentions so that we're not doing it for unhealthy, external status-seeking reasons. Personally speaking, status-seeking is addicting and delivers a false sense of well-being, driven by a hunger for the outside approval of others. Our motivation as entrepreneurs must come from deep within, what renowned researchers and psychologists Ryan and Deci called "intrinsic motivation," when developing their Self-Determination theory.[22] Their theory argues that intrinsic motivations, versus an extrinsic motivation such as status seeking, will almost always bring about the most lasting positive change in people.

Trying to get noticed so others pay attention to you is like eating a bowl of sugary cereal for all three meals in a day—it leaves you hungry and empty. You'll never thrive.

Frequently, entrepreneurs seek status, but that's not a long-term motivator. We must find that which feeds our soul and gives us intrinsic motivation and purpose.

Actor Jim Carrey once said in an interview that early on in his acting career he believed making one more film or getting one more hit would be enough to fulfill him. However, he always wound up emotionally disappointed, no matter how well things went. The experience taught him a great deal, and he revealed his advice to those seeking status:

*I think everybody should get rich and famous and everything they
ever dreamed of, so they can see that that's not the answer.*[23]

Status-seeking is not the answer. We must aim for something
greater than fame and acclaim in order to create meaningful clarity
in our lives.

EntreClarity Run: Clarity on Your Next Breakaway

Imagine a day of the Tour De France, as cyclists from all over
the world compete in the world's most prestigious and difficult
of all bike races, covering 2,235 miles over three weeks. Racers
fill the roads in their brightly colored uniforms and cycle across
the French landscape in search of victory. The riders appear as a
well-orchestrated pack, gliding in unity over the roads. All of a
sudden, a rider, or group of riders, pulls ahead, leaving the others
behind.

This sudden acceleration in cycling, also known as a "breakaway," is when a rider breaks away from the rest of the pack. They
do so to put distance between their bike and the other riders, thus
setting up a potential win for themselves and their team. Within a
cycling race, there can be multiple breakaways. Think of it as the
push that gives you enough momentum to move forward. It's not
the race itself, but these bursts of movement that get us where we
need to go.

For the entrepreneur, the "breakaway" is when you do something that moves you away from your past and towards a more
positive future self, thus enhancing your life with more clarity,

ultimately aligning your Guiding Truths with your future break-aways. For example, you could distance yourself from things that leave you feeling drained and numb, such as a toxic relationship. Or perhaps you've found yourself still in the midst of a bad habit you swore you would break months ago. By eliminating the negative things that don't serve you and stall potential progress towards fulfilling your goals, you're one step closer to a prize far more rewarding. Just as the cycling breakaway sets you up to win the race, you set yourself up for success for the rest of your "race." You're physically, mentally, or emotionally leaving behind the old and all its negativity for a refreshing beginning. You can breathe again. That's clarity.

Interestingly, some of the best breakaways in cycling happen with a small group of peers who breakaway with you. They help you gain distance from the pack even faster and with more power than you could on your own. This is why EntreConnections, one of the eight laws, should be incorporated into each breakaway.

The breakaway is ultimately about YOU and who you want to BECOME. They are the means of living out your Guiding Truths, in real time!

Unlike in cycling, for the entrepreneur, the purpose of a break-away is not to cross the finish line first but to wrestle with a stranger, to engage in mortal combat, to risk yourself, and to care more deeply about your relationship with the process than how it all turns out. A breakaway gives you the opportunity to change and grow by doing something difficult, something you know will cost you. As we push ourselves to our own breakaway, we'll come to find the experience is as important as the end result.

Breakaways are most impactful when they help make Guiding Truths a constant reality in our lives. You should be able to tie all your breakaways to some element of your Guiding Truths. Especially if you want the breakaway to have a lasting positive impact.

Selecting Breakaways That Fuel Thriving

Not all breakaways are created equal. Some breakaways will fuel your thriving more than others, and those are the ones we want to focus our energy on. As you select your top two or three breakaways, ask yourself the following questions to determine which ones will lead to greater thriving:

1. Will this breakaway help me break free from my current undesirable behaviors, relationships, etc.?

2. What story will I be able to tell once this breakaway is complete? Is it a story aligned with my Guiding Truths?

3. Am I doing this breakaway to raise my status or popularity? If yes, own it and ask why. Try to think of a bigger purpose beyond just status.

4. Will the *effort* of the breakaway be challenging/uncomfortable for me and those involved? If not, then you aren't truly breaking away.

5. Do the intended results of the breakaway create excitement and energy?

6. Is this breakaway fueled by love (for myself and others)?

7. How will this breakaway affect those around me, positively and negatively?

8. Are there people around me who can help this breakaway become more successful? Who?

9. Are there people around me who can help this breakaway become more successful? Who?

EntreClarity FLY: Self-Actualize Your New Identity

During the spring of my wife's freshman year in high school, she learned there was one last PE credit required of her that year. It was either that or she could join the track team instead. While Heather had never considered track before, the prospect of taking another PE class seemed out of the question. Squaring her shoulders, she decided to be brave and try something new. Her dad was a good sprinter in high school, and if genetics were on her side maybe she had that same potential, so she planned on signing up for shorter distance runs, such as the 100m and 200m.

Heather summed up the experience by noting that she was hardworking and committed, but only a mediocre sprinter. Even though she had met new people and stepped out of her comfort zone, the lackluster experience left her unsure if she wanted to sign up for track the following year.

Then, another new opportunity crossed her path—some of the girls who ran longer races, such as the one- and two-mile, mentioned that she should join them in the fall for the cross-country team. While she'd heard of cross-country skiing before, she had never heard of cross-country running. Heather didn't know anyone who had ever done any long-distance running. To her young, fifteen-year-old mind, that kind of running was reserved for extreme fitness gurus or people trying to lose weight. However, she faced her fear and as a sophomore, she found herself one of the newest members of the cross-country team.

Distance running opened up a new world to Heather—one where she could see continuous improvement. During her junior year, she met a young adult who had run for a year in college before taking another path in life. Prior to this meeting, she had never even considered the possibility of earning a scholarship and running for a collegiate team. It was as though a lightbulb had turned on in her mind and heart, and she made it her goal to have her college degree paid for by a running scholarship. The running scholarship was now her big goal.

With renewed purpose and clarity for what she wanted to accomplish, she focused on specific training goals. She had an excellent coach who supported and taught her what it took to become the best version of herself on the track. His encouragement opened her eyes to just how much she was capable of achieving. Using this self-actualization, Heather visualized herself winning the race ahead of women she'd never outrun before.

Before drifting off to sleep at night, she implemented this newfound visualization, harnessing the confidence and courage to mentally run through the state cross-country championship race.

THE LAW OF ENTREPRENEURIAL CLARITY: ENTRECLARITY

She would picture where she would be at each mile and exactly how the race would unfold. This visualization didn't come naturally, and she had to fight away doubt and insecurity whenever they tried to creep in.

With this expanded vision, she sought to become the first girl to reach the finish line at the state championship race. At the time, she was perhaps a top ten runner in the state but had not yet beaten the girl whom everyone believed would win the championship. Yet, Heather knew that by winning the state championship, she would secure a college scholarship. The goal was the scholarship, the breakaway to get there was winning the title of state champion. With the weight of a scholarship on her shoulders, she fought against imposter syndrome and other obstacles holding her back. She knew she could do this. Any doubt that said otherwise was simply wrong. Leading up to the race, Heather focused on her progress, not her failures.

October 24, 1990, is a date etched into my wife's memory. On that day, all of the physical and mental training, along with the support of her coach, teammates, and most importantly, her family and faith in God came together. Just as she had visualized, she was first to cross the finish line at the state championship race. She did it! She came from behind and won.

Her once lofty goal became a reality as she received college scholarships and ran all four years for two Division I universities. Being able to compete at the NCAA Cross-Country Championships with her team along with numerous track and cross-country conference championship team titles was rewarding to be a part of. I also found some benefit from her dreams made reality as we shared a college campus. We met and married and, twenty-seven years later, her athletic abilities continue to impress me.

Perhaps unknowingly, Heather practices what psychologist Dr. Gabriele Oettingen calls WOOP.[24] WOOP is a process of what Oettingen labeled as "mental contrasting," and stands for Wishes, Outcome, Obstacles, Plan. In her book, *Rethinking Positive Thinking*, Oettingen uses WOOP as a way to take one's fantasies and dreams and ground them in reality.[25] Thus, helping the dreamer distill it down and create motivation to act. This is what Heather did with her state championship race. Her wish was to win a race that to many, including her, seemed impossible due to the competition that she had struggled against up until then. However, she took that wish, outlined her desired outcome, mentally considered all the obstacles that would keep her from it and how to overcome them, and then developed a clear plan to achieve her wish. Those steps provided her confidence and a reasonable chance of achieving her breakaway of winning the state championship. This is self-actualization at its finest.

You can apply this same methodology, WOOP, in our own breakaways. Distill your breakaways so that the self-actualization of your plan makes the impossible possible.

Self-Actualization and Identity

Abraham Maslow, the American psychologist famous for his hierarchy of needs, believed the highest level of human need was that of self-actualization. Self-actualization is a state of mind that allows individuals to achieve their fullest state of being.[26] It is in that mindset that we find a new identity.

To self-actualize, we must not only think we can do it. We must take on a new identity. We need to adopt the new identity our breakaway is pushing us to be. This identity can often be associated with groups we admire and want to emulate, thus giving us further intrinsic motivation and a sense of belonging. This is what has come to be known as the Social Identity Theory, developed by researchers Henri Tajfel and John Turner and occurs when one adopts certain norms and behaviors from a group that can serve as motivators and fulfill our need to belong.[27]

For instance, when I signed up for my first LoToJa bike race (206 miles in a day), I immediately bought my first road bike the same day. And with that purchase came my new identity.

I was a cyclist.

However, it didn't stop there. Not only was I a cyclist, I was an endurance cyclist. I had a new positive identity that boosted my self-esteem. I felt like I belonged to an elite group of individuals who were total beasts, at least from my perspective! To ensure this identity would stick, I would repeat these words, "I am an endurance cyclist," to myself and others. When people would ask me what I was up to, I usually tried to fit in "...oh, and I became an endurance cyclist since the last time I saw you." Thus, further solidifying my new identity to others. It was empowering!

I believe this new positive identity was the number one reason I finished my first LoToJa only five months after buying a road bike! That is the power of identity.

However, word of caution relative to the Social Identity Theory. Be clear on the identity you want first and then define the group. Some groups' norms and behaviors may not be worth adopting.

Before we move onto your Breakaway Narrative™, it is vital you understand the dark side of identity. Recently I was speaking with a long-time friend of mine, Peter Droubay, who is a professional speaker and sales trainer. Peter has presented on stages thousands of times over his career. After some of his presentations, he's had people come up, congratulate him on a wonderful presentation, and then express to him that they, too, are a "public speaker." Peter, who is a very engaging and present person, will get excited and ask them about their background in public speaking. In almost every case, they may have given a couple of public speeches over the years, but that doesn't make them a public speaker.

When we take on a new identity, we MUST take massive action and lean into that identity. Similarly to my endurance cyclist identity. I took massive action. Within a week of receiving my bike, I completed my first thirty-mile ride. If I had not taken massive action and continued to tell people I was an "endurance cyclist," not only would that have had very little meaning but likely it would have had a negative impact on who I was as a person. Internally, I would have felt like a fraud. This is different from the commonly cited *imposter syndrome*. Imposter syndrome is when we feel we are undeserving of our success, even when we have put in our best efforts.

Identity without our best efforts is just a false identity. We are incongruent with who we say we are. In EntreConnections, we will go deeper into the principle of congruence, which is really what leaning into your identity is all about. When you take on a new identity, strive for that congruence and it will not only boost your confidence but also deepen your most important relationships.

When we know who we are and take massive action to lean into that belief, it brings empowerment to our lives. With a newfound identity, once lofty goals seem achievable. The impossible suddenly appears possible. Just as my wife envisioned her success, believed in her potential, and achieved her dream, we must do the same.

Put on your new identity. Visualize your successful breakaway. Then take massive action to make it happen. You've got this!

The Breakaway Narrative

A Breakaway Narrative is an effective way of taking massive action towards a desired identity and brighter future. As Rami M. Shapiro noted, "The stories we tell ourselves about ourselves determine the quality of the selves we imagine we are."[28]

Take one of your breakaways and write out a narrative for it. By doing so, you write the story of your new identity. You are one step closer to making this dream a reality.

At EntreThrive, we have created a Breakaway Narrative outline template as part of our *EntreClarity Guide* that you can download by visiting **EntreThrive.com/Resources.**

Here is the summary of this powerful breakaway tool:

1. Review your Guiding Truths and identify where this breakaway aligns with it.

2. Turn your Breakaway Narrative into a one sentence statement, phrased as an outcome.

3. List a few mile markers that you must get to for the breakaway to be declared successful.

4. Identify the characters (the Whos) you need to breakaway with you. What do you need to communicate to them?

5. What headwinds might get in the way of the breakaway?

6. What actions will you take to break down these headwinds and move past them?

7. Write out the new identity required to achieve the breakaway, such as "I am an endurance cyclist."

8. Finally, identify your *catalytic mechanism.*

I complete this breakaway exercise when I need clarity on my next Breakaway. Below is a Breakaway Narrative example, using the same questions in the EntreClarity Guide (EntreThrive.com/Re sources):

1. The Breakaway Statement: We will launch a new product offering by the end of the year, powered by AI, that generates $1 million in annual recurring revenue within the next twenty-four months.

2. Does this Breakaway align with my Guiding Truths? If so, how?: Guiding Truth: My ventures create freedom and my life is filled with abundance. This offering must create freedoms for my family, team members, and customers.

3. The Breakaway Drafting Team (list the teammates who will help this breakaway be successful): My COO, AI third-party development team, Marketing Manager

4. Breakaway Desired Outcomes: Build a recurring revenue product, powered by AI, that helps our customers create positive cultures of retention.

5. Your new positive identity you need to adopt—I am an AI pioneer in the homecare industry.

6. Breakaway Headwinds/Obstacles (some examples):

   o Lack of feedback from potential users

   o Poorly designed AI strategy

   o Complexity, hard to use interface

   o Perfection mindset, slowing time to market

7. Breakaway Milemarkers/What must happen (some examples):

   o Detailed milestones/dates outlined—March 1st

   o Customer Focus Group—March 15th

   o AI product strategy/process map—Apr 1st

   o Prototype tested by focus group, focused on simplicity—July 15th

○ Pilot launch to 20 customers—Sept 1st

○ Nationwide launch—Jan 15th

8. Breakaway Catalytic Mechanism: Invest the $100,000 upfront, non-refundable, required to begin the prototype build.

The Catalytic Mechanism

Include in your Breakaway Narrative a catalytic mechanism. This term, originated by Jim Collins, is a device that turns lofty dreams into a reality.[29] It is the link between your breakaway and achieving the breakaway. It is one decision that decides the rest of your decisions.

In the example above, the Catalytic Mechanism is making a $100,000, non-refundable investment in the development of the AI prototype, forcing this entrepreneur to go all-in on her breakaway.

For example, if my breakaway was to achieve a certain finishing time in an upcoming cycling race, my catalytic mechanism could be: Rather than register as a rider (which is what I have done the last four times), register as a racer. Racers are required to stay together and not ride with the slower riders. This catalytic mechanism forces me to train harder or I could get "dropped" by the faster racers and not finish at all.

Whatever your breakaway, you want a catalytic mechanism. You want something that forces you to stick with it and makes giving up seem out of the question. By putting a catalytic mechanism into place, you nearly guarantee your result.

Breakaways Bring You Closer to the Good Life

The last element of Seligman's PERMA model is Accomplishment. Defined by Seligman, this element brings feelings of achievement and mastery.[30] Entrepreneurs find meaning in accomplishment because so much of our work is tied to growth and moving things forward. Accomplishing the impossible gives us positive emotions, the first element of PERMA. Therefore, accomplishment is key to entrepreneurial thriving.

Therefore, to create your Good Life, committing to breakaways throughout your journey can fuel motivation and happiness, under any circumstances. Relating back to my Alaska trip, breakaways can help us find joy in catching the proverbial "fish," even in a downpour.

To truly soar, you must be all-in and totally committed to your breakaway. This means commitment to both the ups and the downs. As Vince Lombardi once said, "Most people fail not because of a lack of desire but because of a lack of commitment."[31]

Cyclists understand the heavy cost of a lack of commitment. If one fails to fully commit during a breakaway, instead of distancing themselves from the other riders in a burst of energy and excitement, they merely fall back into the pack. Sometimes they can fall behind the pack after a poorly executed breakaway. To fail to commit is to fail.

Lean In and Take Action

EntreClarity begins with creating your Guiding Truths, which is the foundation to everything else we will address in this book. First, we crawl by creating Guiding Truths that direct our decisions that cultivate the creation of the Good Life.

Then we walk by being self-aware and accepting who we are today. Self-acceptance causes us to positively evaluate who we are and accept both our strengths and our weaknesses, knowing we can change.

Next, we run by deciding on our breakaways. Breakaways enable us to truly break away from our current self and move toward a bigger, better version of ourselves. Your breakaway could include participation in an Iron Man or starting a second business. Do the breakaway discovery exercise to help you home in on your dreams and goals. Regardless of your breakaway, challenge yourself to become more than who you are today. Remember, they are the important tool that helps us live out our Guiding Truths.

We begin to fly as we self-actualize and commit to our breakaways. During self-actualization, we believe we can reach our full potential and visualize our new, greater identity. Decide on one breakaway and write out your Breakaway Narrative to bring your new identity to life. Finally, we soar when we fully commit to our breakaway.

Next Actions

1. Complete your Guiding Truths, frame it, and keep it top of mind. Go to our free tool at **EntreThrive.com/Reso urces**, for help.

2. Decide on your next Breakaway and fill out the Breakaway tool. Tie it to your new Guiding Truths. Go to **EntreT hrive.com/Resources** to download this tool.

Reflection Questions

Did you truly invest the hours, sometimes days, necessary to create Guiding Truths that you're deeply excited about?

Do your Guiding Truths help you focus on your desired future self and will they help you uncover future breakaways?

Where are you when it comes to EntreClarity? Have you begun to crawl? Are you walking? Running? Flying?

What is something about yourself that you have a hard time accepting? Why?

What breakaway are you most excited about?

Did you download the Breakaway Narrative template and create your first documented breakaway? No? Download it now at **EntreThrive.com/Resources.**

In summary, EntreClarity is about creating what the Good Life could look like. Your personal vision of it. Next up is another essential step of flourishing—the Law of EntreCreate.

The Science Behind the Law of EntreClarity and How It Can Help You to Create Your Good Life

The entrepreneurial journey starts with ideation, a spark that ignites innovation and ambition. However, true accomplishment stems from aligning these ideas with your values, purpose, and identity.

By rooting your entrepreneurial endeavors in the bedrock of your values and purpose, you buffer stress but also recruit the vital energy needed to conquer the unpredictable landscape of business.

EntreClarity can enhance your well-being by:

- **Fueling accomplishment (the A in PERMA model of well-being[22]).**

Aligning work with personal values fosters intrinsic motivation and passion, which is related to self-determination theory.[23]

The theory explains that entrepreneurs who are driven by their values are more likely to experience a sense of enjoyment, engagement, and satisfaction in their work, thereby contributing to enhanced well-being. In fact, several studies indicate that intrinsic motivation is associated with better learning, performance, and well-being.[24]

- **Elevating a stronger sense of purpose and meaning is associated with improved psychological and physical health such as reduction in chronic diseases.**

Entrepreneurs who live in accordance with their values are more likely to report a stronger sense of purpose and meaning in their life.[25]

Research indicates the latter is associated with greater resilience and a reduction in stress and chronic diseases such as heart disease, stroke, and Alzheimer's disease.[26]

- **Protecting one's health.**

People with a clearer sense of purpose are more motivated to pursue preventative health care strategies, which can contribute to more favorable health outcomes and increased longevity.[27]

- **Eliciting greater self-awareness of one's strengths and shortcomings aids in understanding oneself better.**

As an entrepreneur understands and accepts themself better, they can have a deeper understanding of their emotions and behaviors as they relate to others. They can have more empathy and effectively communicate, both of which are foundational social skills in helping build strong and fulfilling relationships. Positive relationships are a key pillar of well-being. Research indicates that happy people have rich and satisfying relationships.[28]

As an entrepreneur understands and accepts themself better, they can have a deeper understanding of their emotions and behaviors as they relate to others. They can have more empathy and effectively communicate, both of which are foundational social skills in helping build strong and fulfilling relationships.

CHAPTER TWO

The Law of Entrepreneurial Creativity: EntreCreate

YOU BELIEVE IN CREATING A BETTER WAY AND A BIGGER WORLD.

Instead of worrying about what you cannot control,
shift your energy to what you can create.
—Roy T. Bennett

When I was young, I was not known among my peers as the creative, artistic type. My drawings, coloring books, and anything identified as "artsy," were not very "artsy." I would color outside the lines and my drawings required translation. Painting? Forget about it. However, coloring outside the lines and drawing unintelligible but creative figures were the first early signs that I was cut out for entrepreneurship. Coloring outside the lines is just another phrase for innovation and creativity. For the entrepreneur, we work best when we are allowed to create without being held back by the limitations others may put on us.

We can struggle with being "artsy," while shining at being creative. Some entrepreneurs can do both really well! I have siblings and children who are entrepreneurs and impressive artists. However, they still create on their own terms and in their own way.

EntreCreate for the entrepreneur follows the same principles. We create better ways because we see beyond the lines and limitations. This is when we are our happiest. When we create, without limitations, we are in what the late renowned positive psychologist, Mihalyi Csikszentmihalyi calls "flow." According to Csikszentmihalyi (pronounced *cheeks-send-me-high*), flow is a state of being that keeps us focused on the present, wrapped in increased creativity, productivity, and joy such that nothing else seems to matter.[39] When I am in flow as an entrepreneur, I am creating something special, accompanied by a perma-grin that remains for the entire day. Flow and creation are synonymous with the other and are key ingredients to creating the Good Life.

The reason that flow is so important for entrepreneurs to access is because research also shows that the happiest and most productive people enter flow states on a regular basis.[40] To break it down, flow, also known as *being in the zone,* occurs when we attempt to meet a challenge that lies just above our skill set. To reach for this goal, we must intensely focus, concentrate, and be free of distractions. As we immerse ourselves fully in the activity, we exert our best effort, and it's not uncommon for us to be less self-aware and lose track of time.

Flow generates such positive emotions like joy, satisfaction, and a sense of accomplishment that it translates into one of the most highly rewarding experiences that an entrepreneur can have. Once we get a taste of this optimal experience, we try to recreate situations where we can enter flow states again and again. So you can see why flow can intrinsically motivate us to keep going and persevering to reach our goals. The creativity generated from flow can act like rewards that help us continue on our path forward despite the difficulties we encounter.

EntreCreate CRAWL: Curiosity Is the Spark that Ignites Creativity

Curiosity is the hallmark of creative people.[41] Their burning curiosity differentiates them from others and provides the interest to persevere long enough in their endeavors to make a significant contribution. In the EntreGrit law, we discuss interest in more depth but here I want to differentiate between the two.

When it comes to ideas and opportunities, curiosity is the spark that draws us in and gets us started, while new knowledge is the kindling that the spark ignites. The combination of curiosity and the knowledge it lights, are the foundational elements of creativity. Entrepreneurs must lead with curiosity in order to start the spark of creativity. This is why curiosity is considered one of twenty-four character strengths identified by respected psychologists Drs. Martin Seligman and Christopher Peterson.[42] Together they undertook an extensive study of various cultures, religions, and philosophical texts to identify universal virtues and strengths. This research culminated in the development of the VIA Classification of Character Strengths and Virtues, of which there are twenty-four strengths and six virtues.

Each strength has been categorized under one of the six virtues. We will cover more about character strengths in EntreHabits, but for now, I want to highlight the fact that curiosity is categorized under the virtue of wisdom. According to the VIA Institute on Character®, to be curious is to explore and uncover new knowledge.[43] Curiosity is what creates greater knowledge and wisdom in our lives. It helps us explore new frontiers.

Would it then surprise you that creativity is also one of the twenty-four character strengths and categorized under the virtue of wisdom? Curiosity and creativity go together like peanut butter and jelly.

Once an idea is ignited, then interest is the wood that keeps the fire going. And the fire? That's the passion that originated from that one spark. But it doesn't stop there. If the fire burns hot and bright enough, then those passions can turn into true callings. More on interest, passions, and callings in the next chapter. My focus here is on the spark, the curiosity. Without it, there is no fire. Nothing can be created without the spark of curiosity.

EntreCreators

Based on the research of Seligman and Peterson and then shared on the VIA website, creativity has two essential components: originality and adaptiveness.[44] When we are in creation mode as entrepreneurs, we are developing ideas that are originally ours and then adaptive or useful. This is the power of entrepreneurial creativity. What we create changes the world! Hopefully, for the better.

Creativity and entrepreneurship go hand-in-hand. Eaton Business School even deems creativity a must-have skill and characteristic for those who seek entrepreneurship.[45] For entrepreneurs, creativity encourages new ways of developing a product or service and brings about innovative and novel ways of doing business. Thinking outside of the box enables the entrepreneur to change the status quo through exploration and innovative problem-solving. Creators change the world.

Entrepreneurs' resilience, self-determination, and innovation fuel their passion to create. This creativity can impact society substantially by positively affecting social, environmental, and financial problems, along with many other issues. For example, Tyler Bosmeny, CEO and co-founder of Clever, uses his EdTech company to change the world by improving education. Bosmeny believes everyone can benefit from a better education, and his company's software provides students with personalized resources based on their specific needs.[46] Entrepreneurs can also help reduce poverty, as their companies provide employment, which leads to a ripple effect. Job creation not only positively impacts the person but his or her community as well.

Entrepreneurs are happiest when they create because it gives them energy and confidence. Conversely, when entrepreneurs fail to create and get caught up in the day-to-day tasks and putting out fires, their well-being suffers. When their creation becomes stagnant, problems in their personal and professional lives blend together, resulting in chaos and mental anguish. The world suffers, too, when their creation comes to a standstill.

Curiosity Leads to Passion and Cultivating Creativity

In 2009, my sister-in-law, Julia Marcum, was a stay-at-home mom in need of a creative outlet. Her curiosity about the fairly new field of DIY design blogs led her to start her own, Chrislovesjulia.com.

As someone who's heavily affected by her surroundings, Julia focused on beautifying her home and posting about it on her blog. In the beginning, her audience included mainly family and friends, but over time, strangers with a shared passion for DIY took interest in her creativity and style.

As her blog grew, Julia pulled in her husband (and my brother) Chris to help with some of her projects. In 2016, Chris left his full-time job, working for me as my then Director of Marketing, to focus on the business side of the blog, giving Julia more time for designing and creating, while caring for her two children. Despite not knowing where their business would take them, their curiosity kept them engaged in this passion project, hoping to turn it into something more than just a creative outlet. In the beginning, it was their curiosity that opened the door to creating something special, encouraging the pair to throw caution to the wind and give it a try. Julia's favorite time to create is when she can find time to go "all-in" and find her own type of flow. When she is creating during flow, she thinks beyond the limits of her industry and what new and innovative products they can bring to the marketplace. This is truly coloring outside the lines!

Today, Chris and Julia have developed one of the most successful DIY home design sites in the world. They have worked with businesses such as Lowe's®, Amazon, Party City®, and Crate&Barrel, have created successful product lines with Pottery Barn® and RubberMaid®, and have built up their own Mastermind Community, *Good Influence*®, an online member community that teaches active influencers how to ethically and organically, monetize their content.

When Julia started the blog in 2009, the possibility of it becoming a full-time job was not on the horizon or even on her mind. Monetized content creation in general was unheard of. For reference, Instagram® had yet to take its place in society. Chrislovesjulia was the first of its kind. Nonetheless, driven by creativity, Julia diligently posted to the blog regardless if people were going to read it or not. There were no deadlines and no big-time names taking their place as her readers, at least not yet. It was her self-proclaimed consistency and love for creation that enabled her to never miss a day of posting quality content to the blog.

While coaching other influencers, Julia notes the key to creation is finding what you love and are called to do. When someone voices their distaste for a particular design, Julia knows she's doing something right. The pushback from others means she's forging her own path and not just giving people what they want.

As a creative entrepreneur, Julia tells others to create what they love, not what they think people will love. To lean into their curiosities, as she did, where passion can be developed and pursued. Julia believes that when you pursue your passions, your audience will find you. But passions are often not discovered but rather pursued, sparked by our curiosity.

As Julia and Chris's story demonstrates, entrepreneurs are creators at heart, and they need key people in their lives to help them find the space to create. Entrepreneurs who only create when it's convenient tend to lose interest and fail to follow through. However, those who can consistently create make the world a better place and personally thrive.

Julia can create because of the role her husband plays in their business. Though an entrepreneur in his own right, Chris taps into his own creative juices by running the backend of the business. Creativity for entrepreneurs is often deployed behind the scenes, in the form of processes and systems. Their partnership perfectly illustrates Dan Sullivan's *Who Not How* mindset of achieving your goals by delegating tasks to others. Chris is Julia's who, and by focusing on running the back end of the business, he gives her the time and freedom to channel her energy into creating, while still staying true to his own need to create and bring value to the partnership.

EntreCreate WALK: The Freedom and Space to Create

Entrepreneurs must have the freedom to create. As busy entrepreneurs who wear many hats and bear many responsibilities, we must make the time in our overpacked schedules to create. To have an impactful outcome, we must set aside the space and freedom in our calendars and set aside time for creation. This means we can't allow the day-to-day fires to get in the way of creating. Whenever we stop creating, not only does our well-being suffer, but so does the work environment we've created.

The freedom to create begins in the mind. To create, we must mentally give ourselves permission to do so—guilt-free. Since creative individuals alternate between imagination and reality, entrepreneurs must be intentional about carving out time to dream and fantasize a world that is different from the one they currently experience.

An entrepreneur's mind can be powerfully imaginative. However, this also presents a caveat. Using one's strength of imagination can lead to envisioning and innovation. But if used incorrectly, it can corrosively lead to imagining a set of obstacles and dire outcomes to occur. Without a plan to identify how to deal with these imagined obstacles, entrepreneurs can fall into all kinds of mind traps that can lead to anxiety, procrastination, and a host of false starts.

That is why it is important for entrepreneurs to foster an agile mind so they can identify what they *wish* for (i.e., their big breakaway) and their desired *outcome*, potential *obstacles* that can occur along the way, and most importantly, a *plan* to deal with these sets of obstacles. Remember WOOP in the last chapter?[47] To successfully incorporate WOOP, entrepreneurs must tap into their creativity and imagination. Dreaming and curiosity is just the beginning of the EntreCreate process. In fact, most of the creation happens after curiosity. Outlining outcomes, obstacles, and plans is when the creativity kicks in.

The last important point relative to planning your creative freedom is to let go of the guilt you might feel when taking time to create a better life for yourself, your family, and your business. In that order. Too often, we get caught up in "busy work" and allow ourselves to feel guilty when we take time to create, because it might not relate to the urgency of the day. To create, you must consistently make the time and put forth the energy to create! When you have a wish and/or dream, creating involves listing the desired outcome, obstacles, and plan. Guilt and shame are the obstacles to some of your greatest outcomes. Plan for it and you will create the impossible.

The Space to Create

After mentally giving yourself the freedom to create, it's time to give yourself the space in your schedule. I recommend freeing up time in the morning. For example, I take all of my appointments in the afternoon because I block out mornings for my creative time. Whenever possible, I also try to keep my appointments to Mondays, which helps free up the rest of my week for creation in general.

The famous singer-songwriter James Taylor describes his songwriting creative process as one that requires isolation. While he may not need many things to write, having a space to create is essential for him. As Taylor once commented, "I think in order to create, artistic people need to be alone. They need to have time to themselves."[48]

In the same way, entrepreneurs also need the space to create. They need time away from all of the distractions and noise. While creative people have a great deal of energy, they are often quiet. Contrary to popular belief, creative people are not always "on." They sleep and take rests when needed. These periods of quiet and idleness are vital to the success of their work.

When entrepreneurs enjoy the space and freedom to create, they are prime to enter into deeper states of creative flow. As Mihaly Csikszentmihalyi writes, "Constant busyness is not a good prescription for creativity."[49] Those who keep themselves busy generally fail to be creative, as having the time to mentally meander is essential to the creative process.

The Divergent Entrepreneur Needs Space

Csikszentmihalyi also authored *Creativity: Flow and the Psychology of Discovery and Invention*. In this book, he differentiates between convergent creation and divergent thinking.[50] Convergent is more measurable, such as via IQ tests, where there is one correct answer, for example, solving a math problem. Divergent thinking is more fluent, less structured, and requires many ideas, perspectives, and identification of associations. Sound familiar? Divergent thinking is creative thinking. For the entrepreneur, I resonate with the term divergent visionaries.

According to Csikszentmihalyi, many of the participants in their research on creativity might have two to three good ideas, but those ideas have kept them busy for a lifetime.[51] Jeff Bezos, who dreamt up Amazon, even today, continues to keep busy and engaged, because his business is constantly changing, flexible, and fluent. His original idea has turned into many, many more that have literally changed the world.

Creating the Good Life for yourself requires divergent thinking. There is never one answer and therefore, tapping into our divergent way of thinking when we are trying to create a better life for ourselves and family, is vital. Our journey to the Good Life must be fluent, flexible, and free. For me personally, when I am practicing divergent thinking on a daily basis, I am experiencing consistent wins that feed my confidence and have led me to some of my greatest ideas that continue to engage me to this day. Csikszentmihaly's team have found that creative people find incredible joy in just the process of creation, and not just the end result. Taking time to tap into our divergent visionary creative side, adds to our well-being and happiness.

Here's a word of caution when it comes to divergent visionaries. According to Csikszentmihalyi's research, creative divergents can also feel isolated and alone, because so many around us think convergently.[52] If you've ever seen the *Divergent* movie series, starring Shailene Woodley, you can likely relate to this. Shailene was considered a "divergent," which was taboo for this future society. Divergents were free thinkers and questioned the status quo. This future society couldn't have that and so when they would find one, they would make them disappear. This is, of course, an exaggeration of my point, but divergents in this context think differently and the world needs us more than ever!

Because divergent thinking is so important to the well-being of an entrepreneur, creating the right kind of space that will get us into deep flow is vital. This creative time and space is part of our rejuvenating process. We step away from the sometimes exhaustive noise and step into a creative space. For me, getting out into nature is the ticket, but I realize that for some of you in the big cities this can be a challenge. Try to get outside, when possible, but at the very least, find a creative space that is quiet and has windows to the outside.

Here's a quick disclaimer: *Be flexible* and prepare for uncertainty. If something unexpected happens, just commit to creating more space for creation! Whenever possible, do your best to move your "uncertainties" to the afternoons. From Tuesday through Friday, I rarely have an appointment with another before noon, unless I am conducting an all-day coaching session or workshop.

EntreCreate RUN: Deep Thrive® Creative Sessions

For at least fifteen years, I've spent time in some form of what I call Deep Thrive Sessions. There are other terms that align with Deep Thrive Sessions, such as Deep Work (Cal Newport), Clarity Breaks (EOS® and Gino Wickman), and Flow (Mihaly Csikszentmihalyi). Though all similar in their desired outcomes, a Deep Thriving Session is 100 percent about creation that brings energy and confidence at the beginning of each day and I strongly recommend you avoid solving specific business issues during these sessions. Deep Thrive sessions create energy and confidence at the beginning of a day.

Before you do anything else in the morning (even exercise), begin your day in a Deep Thriving Session, as it will enable you to start your day with confidence. By entering into a Deep Thriving Session, we create the space, the time, and the stillness for creation. As Eckhart Tolle said, "Stillness is where creativity and solutions to problems are found."[53]

Deep Thriving Begins with Meditation

Begin your Deep Thriving Session with meditation. Earlier this year, I decided to go deeper with my meditation and attended a meditation retreat at *The Art of Living Retreat Center* (artoflivin gretreatcenter.org), just outside of Boone, NC. It was a life-changing experience for me and one that I would recommend to anyone who wants to go deeper with their meditation practice. The type of meditation they teach is Sudarshan Kriya, nicknamed SKY, which is a formalized breathing technique, using specific breathing rhythms, designed to get one unstuck and foster presence. This wonderful practice was created years ago by the center's founder, the world-renowned spiritual leader Gurudev Sri Sri Ravi Shankar, known by many as Sri Sri.

Since adopting SKY as my primary meditation practice, I have found a deeper sense of awe, focus, and presence in my daily life. However, SKY is best learned at the center due to its technical and precise nature. If learning SKY is not in your future, there are several apps and mindfulness meditation techniques that you can incorporate. However, not all are helpful for the busy-minded entrepreneur. Find meditation practices that support creativity and focus. This is not a book on meditation and I am not an expert, therefore, do your research and find one that frees and expands your mind.

Prayer: Making Intentions for Inspiration

As I meditate, I also gain the focus to pray. I find my prayers are clearer and more specific after meditation. As a Christian, I ask for inspiration from Christ and the Holy Spirit to help me create. However, no matter your faith, prayer is universal and an excellent way to connect to the ultimate Creator, God, who can inspire our creations. Feel free to tweak the following prayer according to your beliefs in a higher power:

Dear [God, Higher Power, etc.], remove all blocks to my creativity. Show me what I should create next. Help me to create something that brings You glory and makes the world a better place. In your name, Amen.

Along with praying for inspiration, pray that whatever you create today will bless the lives of those you serve. This kind of selfless prayer has often led to greater inspiration. If prayer is not in the cards for you, try reading something inspiring, like a positive quote or paragraph in a book. Whatever might help create positive emotions before you enter into your creative mindset.

Creative Journaling

After meditation and prayer, take the time for creative journaling. Begin by writing down three things you envision will bring you gratitude during the day ahead. Here, you aren't looking back at what you accomplished the day before, but you are looking *forward* and creating gratitude for the near future. I use the evenings to write down my grateful moments of the day.

Gratitude is an essential part of sparking creativity. Studies have demonstrated a link between gratitude and creative problem-solving, as our positive emotions increase our ability to solve problems and come up with new, fresh ideas.[54]

Next, write one to two creative outcomes you'd like to accomplish by the end of your Deep Thriving Session. These can be personal, relationship outcomes, topics you want to learn more about, planning a family vacation, focusing on a Character Strength you want to hone, etc.

Your creative outcomes for a Deep Thriving Session should always be focused on creation. This is your time as an entrepreneur to awaken your best creative self. Take advantage of this creation time before you become too distracted with running your business and the day-to-day tasks.

The Deep Thrive Guide

By going to **EntreThrive.com/Resources**, you can download the free guide to Deep Thrive Sessions. This guide goes over best practices to make these sessions meaningful, creative, and energizing. Additionally, using the Breakaway Narrative tool, also at **EntreT hrive.com/Resources**, during a Deep Thrive session, can be very useful.

EntreCreate FLY: Take Action

This past year, I attended and spoke at the International World Congress for Positive Psychology in Vancouver, British Columbia, put on by the International Positive Psychology Association (IPPA). If you ever want to see what it's like to be surrounded by hundreds of some of the most genuine and service-minded people on Earth, attend an IPPA conference. I had the pleasure of meeting Tricia Fox Ransom, a fellow alum of my MAPP program at the University of Pennsylvania, and an accomplished singer and songwriter. Tricia and my classmate Paula Toledo, and another well-known MAPP alum, Shannon Polly, gave a great presentation on music and its impact on well-being. I quickly became fascinated with Tricia's work with the organization, Purple Songs Can Fly, whose mission is to help children receiving pediatric cancer treatment at the Texas Children's Cancer and Hematology Center, creatively write their own songs. Tricia helps bring this mission to fruition by facilitating songwriting sessions with these wonderful kids. Inspired by her story, I had to learn more and interviewed Tricia a couple of weeks later.

She shares the story of a young boy, diagnosed with terminal cancer with little time to live, and how the creative process of making his own songs helped him live for an entire year longer. He loved to create and write songs about love, and for him, that creative process helped him get through more treatments and the physical struggles he had to endure. Though he passed away, his quality of life was elevated because he had space to create with Tricia's guidance.

I was struck by what the creative process of helping these children write songs has also done for Tricia. As she facilitates this powerful exercise with them, she also taps into her divergent thinking process and finds joy in being their creative guide. This type of connection, fueled by creativity, unifies, and deepens relationships.

We all have this kind of unifying creativity within us as entrepreneurs. We make the world a better place when our creations are focused on just that. Like Tricia, we are also the happiest when we are creating, and it is almost impossible for that happiness to stay only with us. The law of EntreCreate is maximized when our creations positively influence our communities, friends, family, and ourselves.

To fly with EntreCreate, we must adopt a selfless approach and share our creations with everyone we can. I have been the recipient of people who have selflessly created, sometimes without receiving anything in return, so that I could benefit. The path to the Good Life is surrounded by creative people.

Next Actions

1. Write down one to three activities and/or business ideas that you've been curious about but never took action on. Identify one and fill out a Breakaway Narrative worksheet (**EntreThrive.com/Resources**) to see if it is something you want to pursue.

2. Schedule your time to create and block it out. Daily, if possible, but at minimum, once a week. Start slowly and work up to two plus hours each session.

3. By going to **https://entrethrive.pro.viasurvey.org/**, you can take the Character Strengths Survey and identify your five key character strengths, spoken of earlier.

The Science Behind the Law of EntreCreate and How It Can Help You to Create Your Good Life

In the world of entrepreneurship, where the demands and challenges are constant, consistently nurturing your well-being is critical to achieving a happy and fulfilling life. The law of EntreCreate serves as a mental reprieve, almost like an intermittent recovery from the highly intense pace that it takes to run a business.

EntreCreate can enhance your well-being through:

Stress reduction and mental health.

Carving out time for mindfulness practices and meditation can support your mental health as studies show that practicing the present-moment experience through mindfulness can be an effective way to reinforce your calmness and stability of your mind. It can be a short-circuit to the fight-or-flight reaction that accompanies stressful situations.[17]

Enhanced problem-solving and innovation.

Making time for active daydreaming, fantasy, imagination, and creativity is a form of play. Studies link play to the psychological state of flow and timelessness, which is associated with greater life satisfaction. Being engrossed in a Deep Thrive session can promote flow and help you to lose your self-consciousness, enhance your focus and concentration, help you to use your skill to meet a challenge, and reward you with positive emotions, like joy, that come from being fully immersed in an activity![18]

Self-expression and self-discovery.

As entrepreneurs, we can become absorbed in the pursuit of our business-related goals. However, if we divert some of our attention and free up creative energy, we will naturally find ourselves in a curious state of exploration. To sustain curiosity, we must learn to enjoy being curious about ourselves and the world around us.[19] Self-expression and self-discovery can increase our self-esteem and confidence as entrepreneurs.

Increased productivity and efficiency. Immersing oneself in acts of self-reflection and solitude can appear counter to the entrepreneur's productive "do-ing" mindset. However, constant busyness is not a good recipe for creativity.[20] Rather, by "being" with ourselves in a way that induces relaxation and creativity, we are harnessing positive emotions like enthusiasm, serenity, interest, awe, and inspiration. These emotions can act like pulleys in reducing the force of the heavy lifting that comes with being an entrepreneur. The end result is greater achievement of goals, higher productivity, and efficiency in all areas of your life.

Chapter Three

The Law of Entrepreneurial Grit: EntreGrit

WHAT YOU FEEL CALLED TO CREATE FUELS YOUR STAYING POWER.

Those fortunate people who do see their work as a calling, as opposed to a job or a career, reliably say "my work makes the world a better place." And it's they who seem most satisfied with their jobs and their lives overall.

—Angela Duckworth, Best-Selling author of Grit

When I entered the in-home care space (caregivers, aides, nurses caring for seniors in the home), perhaps I was a little naive to undertake such a venture at a young age. I quickly noticed I was half the age of many people in the industry and senior care tended to attract older owners. Most of my peers had many, many years on me, and I knew I faced an uphill battle.

I needed grit.

Grit is truly about perseverance and staying power in the face of adversity. Grit stays on track and refuses to move off course, no matter how dire the circumstances. Going back to the law of EntreCreate, EntreGrit starts first with the spark, curiosity. Interest, knowledge, passion, and a calling are possible only when we act on our curiosities. However, to avoid redundancy, just know that curiosity sparks our interest. More on these two principles later.

When starting my home-care agency, I had an interest centered around having an impact and helping seniors age gracefully, away from the hospital. This interest led me to get out of corporate America, so I could do something that I felt truly made a difference.

Chasing this interest eventually led me to practice my craft more, which deepened my passion for it, and, ultimately, led me to my calling of solving quality in-home care standards for an entire industry. Deepening grit for an entrepreneur doesn't come overnight. My interest found deeper meaning and evolved into a passion for wanting to make a greater impact beyond what I was currently doing. My Breakaway was turning my passion into a calling, which became the staying power, my EntreGrit. I went from home-care owner, my passion, to elevating in-home care for millions of seniors in North America, my calling at that point in m y life.

When you are called, grit will find you and give you the needed lift. It will pull you through challenges that passion alone may not be enough to solve. The law of EntreGrit stretches beyond passion and is fueled by what you feel called to create. Someone who truly incorporates the law of EntreGrit, understands staying power is deepened when they feel a calling to do their work.

The question to ask yourself is where are you relative to the progression of entrepreneurial grit? Are you in the curiosity, interest, practice, passion, or calling phase of your journey?

Below is a simple illustration that outlines my five levels of EntreGrit. As you can see, EntreGrit grows stronger as you work towards the calling phase. The 1–10 scale is simply to show the potential impact each level can have on deepening grit and is not based on any specific research study.

THE 5 LEVELS OF
ENTREGRIT

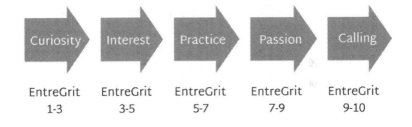

Curiosity	Interest	Practice	Passion	Calling
EntreGrit 1-3	EntreGrit 3-5	EntreGrit 5-7	EntreGrit 7-9	EntreGrit 9-10

EntreGrit CRAWL: Planting the Seed

To grow in grit, we must first plant the seed by understanding our Guiding Truths, as described in the first law, EntreClarity. Angela Duckworth uses the term *life philosophy*, but the two concepts are well-aligned. A life philosophy is simply what you're trying to get out of life. It's your ultimate concern. As Duckworth explains, our grit "grows as we figure out our life philosophy."[59] Conversely, if we lack goals, especially an ultimate goal we are trying to achieve, that can result in a lack of grit.[60]

For entrepreneurs to develop their own EntreGrit, it is important to develop and document your Guiding Truths. Refer to the EntreClarity law if you have not already done so. By aligning your Guiding Truths with your curiosity, interest, and passion, you are setting yourself up for a deeper calling as an entrepreneur.

If we know passion is what fuels our perseverance, eventually leading to our calling, it is essential to pinpoint what we truly want out of life. If you lack passion, you will lack perseverance. And without perseverance, you will not feel called and therefore will lack the grit needed to EntreThrive.

Consider Kobe Bryant, one of the most successful basketball players of all time. When Bryant was on the Olympic Team USA, he began his conditioning work around 4:30 a.m., continued to run and sprint until 6 a.m., lifted weights until 7 a.m., and then would make eight hundred jump shots until 11 a.m.[61] Finally, he joined the rest of Team USA for their 11 a.m. practice. It's no wonder Kobe Bryant won five NBA championships and two Olympic gold medals. He was devoted to practice, which quickly added to his knowledge, leading to passion, and I have no doubt he felt called to his craft.

EntreGrit WALK: Turn Interest Into Passionate Persistence

Colin O'Brady understands his passion—to do the impossible. This passion gives him the grit needed for his phenomenal feats. In December 2019, O'Brady made history as part of a six-man team who rowed across the Drake Passage—six hundred miles of ocean water from the southern tip of South America to Antarctica.[62] The trek required him to row every ninety minutes for twelve days straight. To accomplish this rowing feat across such unpredictable and treacherous waters, O'Brady needed to perform mentally and physically at high levels.

While he had already made history in 2018 by becoming the first person to cross the Antarctic land mass alone and fueled by his own power, the Drake passage was different—O'Brady would face the water this time, and he had never rowed a boat until three months prior to the task.

What enabled O'Brady to succeed? How did he achieve the seemingly impossible? How did he make history yet again?

It started with his interest, which turned into passionate persistence, which kept him pushing forward to accomplish the impossible. He has grit.

O'Brady has the willingness to do hard things. Consider the grueling 3 a.m. training sessions to prepare for the Drake Passage, where he immersed himself in ice-cold water and used other unorthodox workouts to prepare himself for anything that came his way.[63] O'Brady has the passion to accomplish the impossible. He understands his goal and possesses a willingness to suffer the pain to reach the payoff. He understands we must experience lows in life—the 1s, 2s, and 3s—to experience the 9s and 10s. O'Brady's life shows how far grit can take you—it's the fuel to accomplish the impossible.

Passion Alone Can Take You Far

My own Drake Passage—or impossible mission— was the first year I ever rode in LoToJa. It was truly my Breakaway to better health. It all started, in 2016, when I desired to get healthy again. I knew running wasn't my passion, but I had biked just enough to know it was a possibility. On April 6, I ordered my first road bike and entered LoToJa, a two hundred-mile bike race. I was determined to get fit and this seemed the way to do it. To be honest, when I registered, it was purely driven by curiosity, which led to a deep interest rather quickly, that biking might have on my own health and well-being. I could not claim passionate persistence at that point.

In those early days, I began wondering what I had gotten myself into. I had never ridden a road bike before. I'd never had to "clip" into pedals before. I was a complete novice and wrecked a time or two in the first couple of months because road biking was so foreign to me. I'd never done anything like this in my life. *Had I made a mistake?*

Fueled by my interest, I continued to train and practice. This practice led to further knowledge of the impact it was beginning to have on my health, which fed my internal drive, my passion. I remember completing my first fifty miles—I felt drained after the experience and found it incredibly difficult. Thankfully, my new passion for biking saw me through the pain of learning how. My passion also provided the fuel I needed to suffer the 1s, 2s, and 3s to experience my own 8s, 9s, and 10s. Before long, I rode one hundred miles and started gaining a sense of accomplishment. I experienced a high, and it seemed to foreshadow what I'd feel after LoToJa.

During this time, I trained with two other buddies, Matt and Brett. Having these two friends with me made the task easier. When you share a passionate goal with someone, your ability to finish the race increases. Brett had also completed LoToJa twice before and having someone along for the ride who had already done it, helped us. While finishing LoToJa seemed impossible, we chased after it anyway.

The day of the race finally arrived. But after one hundred fifty miles into it, I wanted to give up, as pain seared through my body from head to toe. I didn't know what to do. How would I finish the last fifty miles? I knew my family was praying and rooting for me to finish. I also knew the journey I had been through and the sacrifices I'd endured to get here. That knowledge pushed me through the final fifty miles.

Matt, Brett, and I all crossed the finish line at the same time. We finished our impossible race together, and I was on cloud nine. I'd never experienced anything like it before and didn't come down for a while afterward.

But the thrill didn't come from crossing the finish line. It came from knowing what we had gone through to get there—all the hours, weeks, and months of training. All the effort it took to accomplish the task. All the grit required for the job.

According to Duckworth, the term passion refers to someone who shows "consistency over time."[64] So, passion is really about how steadily you hold onto your goals over time. Those who have passion aren't seeking something fresh because of novelty. They aren't looking for change. Instead, they consistently work toward a definite goal and tend to stay on task. People with grit have this kind of passion. As Duckworth notes, "Enthusiasm is common. Endurance is rare."[65]

Passion, however, is often found only after we've put in the work. Unfortunately, many "self-help" experts have used terms such as, "just follow your passions," or "your passion will find you." Though I'm sure there have been some who have known their passions immediately, most of us are not that lucky. I have never been that lucky.

Passion requires acting on curiosity, interest, and practice. To be willing to put in the work. Once we have, then we are far more prepared to choose whether we are passionate about whatever we've pursued, or not. In this day and age of instant gratification, we have, unfortunately, fallen prey to thinking passion will manifest itself early on as we pursue our curiosity, skipping levels 2 and 3. At least for me, the things I have become most passionate about took a whole lot of practice, learning, and digging into.

Once we do find our passion, impossible breakaways become possible. Passion is a key ingredient to creating the Good Life. However, like I mentioned earlier, there are some obstacles we face that passion alone may not solve.

EntreGrit RUN: What You Feel Called to Create Fuels Your Staying Power

Curiosity, interest, practice, purpose, passion. All these levels of EntreGrit lead you to the ultimate staying power, your calling. Through my own experiences, setbacks, and confronting fear in the face; EntreGrit, to me, is always more effective when there is a calling to back it up. My definition of an entrepreneurial calling is when our passion turns into a selfless act of solving problems that change the world for the better.

Another way to understand EntreGrit is to consider what it isn't. EntreGrit isn't talent, luck, or a fleeting passion for something. As Duckworth explains,

Grit is about having what some researchers call an "ultimate concern"—a goal
you care about so much that it organizes and gives meaning to almost everything
you do.[66]

This sounds quite like a calling. Callings give meaning to almost everything we do. Your "ultimate concern," your calling, is the pinnacle ingredient of EntreGrit.

Let me give you a real-life personal example that illustrates all these phases of grit, eventually leading to what I currently believe I am called to do.

1. My crawl started with my *curiosity* and then *interest* in positive psychology, the science of well-being, and how it could help me find deeper meaning in my personal and professional life. This interest led me to read *The Happiness Advantage: The Seven Principles of Positive Psychology That Fuel Success and Performance at Work* by Shawn Achor.

2. Once I completed the book, I began to *practice* the principles I was learning from the field of positive psychology and apply them. Facing many obstacles and uncertainties along the way, my practice and interest helped me find enough grit to push through and develop better habits, clarity, creativity, and overall well-being for myself. Seeing the benefits, my interest and practice began to turn into a passion to help my fellow entrepreneurs.

3. My walk commenced when I began to be *passionate* about learning more, which led me to apply to the top Masters of Applied Positive Psychology program in the world. Upon acceptance, participation furthered my learning, specifically in my area of interest of entrepreneurial well-being. This program was extremely challenging because I had not been in school for twenty-five years.

This passion helped me get through the late study nights, relentless assignments, all while running multiple businesses, building a home, and spending less time with my family. Squeezing an additional 25–30 hours of study into each week was one of the most challenging times of my life.

4. After more practice, learning, and feeding my passion, I began to turn my passion into a true calling of helping entrepreneurs live a better life, the Good Life. I am now in the running phase of EntreGrit, where my passion has turned into a calling, all of which is tied to my Guiding Truths.

By nature, I prefer to stay out of the public eye and just grow businesses, but because writing this book and growing the EntreThrive community has turned into a calling, I have learned to embrace getting comfortable with the uncomfortable. I am willing to push myself into frontiers I have not yet explored, such as writing this book, being on podcasts, and putting myself out there to help fulfill what I now feel called to do.

The Dangers of Callings: Obsessive vs. Harmonious

One point of caution as you work towards finding your own calling if you haven't already. Just because you feel called, doesn't mean you won't burnout out and/or burn out the people around you! In a recent study of 326 entrepreneurs, researchers identified two types of passion, obsessive and harmonious.[67] Here is a summary of how the researchers defined each:

- *Obsessive passion*, where one obsesses about their work and calling, whatever that might be, at the expense of spending time with those they love and pursuing other passions. If an activity does not involve their work, its importance in their life diminishes. This is a dangerous path to burnout.

- *Harmonious passion,* on the other hand, is tied to enjoyment of their work, with the freedom to engage with it or not. They can step away from it, spending time on other passions, without feeling the guilt, conflict, and shame that obsessive passionate entrepreneurs often feel.

I have experienced both sides of this kind of passion, while still feeling called to make an impact with my work. In fact, full transparency, writing this book has sometimes put me in an obsessive passionate state, where I would feel guilty stepping away from it. More recently, my love for cycling has sometimes taken a backseat to writing this book. When I did cycle, I would find myself conflicted on whether riding my bike was the best use of my time or if I should be home writing. I am a bit embarrassed admitting to feeling that way. Of course, riding my bike, often with my wife, was the best thing I could be doing at the time, but due to my obsessive passion, some of those rides were not as enjoyable as they should have been. My mind was back at my office, feeling guilty for not working on this book. Another example of when I allowed obsessive passion to overtake me was when I was under my desk, working on the industry benchmarking study. I was certainly burned out, even though I felt called to do the work.

As passionate entrepreneurs, we can fall prey to obsessive passion easily, especially when we feel called. So, be mindful of how you approach your passion and calling with your entrepreneurial venture. For example, if you have a difficult time separating your work from your personal life on the weekends, you might be experiencing an obsessive passion that may eventually lead to burnout and rob you of your EntreGrit. Make space and time for your most important connections, interests, and passions. Freeing your weekends from work is a great start, and then Deep Thrive Sessions, covered in EntreCreate, also give you space to pursue other passions and find meaning in creation.

Evaluate Your EntreGrit

Take time to evaluate where you're at when it comes to your EntreGrit. If you are still in the interest phase, outline a path that will move you effectively towards the practice, passion, and calling phases. It is important to note here that there may be times when an interest has plateaued! Significant effort can be wasted on curiosities and interests that we keep hoping will turn into passions. Consistently evaluate and be willing to walk away if your interest seems stagnant, no matter how much sincere practice and/or effort you have put in.

Entrepreneurship is not for the faint of heart. It requires enormous personal and professional sacrifices. Additionally, entrepreneurs have often risked their hard-earned savings, a secure job, and so much more to start a new venture.

What would cause an individual to leave a reliable job and sign up for a life of blood, sweat, and tears?

They have grit—the passion and the perseverance to take on a challenge. By achieving their goals, entrepreneurs can increase their confidence and self-efficacy; ignite positive emotions such as joy, interest, pride, and inspiration; and improve their well-being. In fact, studies show that grit is associated with positive affect, happiness, and life satisfaction.[68]

In the end, grit provides staying power and is essential to those who desire to EntreThrive.

Next Actions

1. From the curiosity list you wrote in the last chapter, evaluate what actions you've taken since and what level of EntreGrit they are in. What is the subsequent step to take to get to the next phase, or do you need to go to the next item on the list? Know when to quit or move to the next level. As a side note, callings usually don't manifest themselves until you reach the passionate phase.

2. Evaluate your current passion(s). Are any of those future callings? If so, what steps do you need to take to get them there?

3. If you feel called right now to something, is it aligned with your new Guiding Truths? If so, why? If not, why? Evaluate what needs to change if there is some misalignment.

Once you establish your passion and your "ultimate concern," you'll discover your calling. This calling will carry you through the difficult times. It will cause you to chase the seemingly impossible. What comes next in the EntreThrive model is deepening your connections. Let's move to the fourth step of flourishing—the Law of EntreConnections.

The Science Behind the Law of EntreGrit and How It Can Help You to Create Your Good Life

Resilience-building. Grit, the psychological trait that involves a person's passion and perseverance for long-term goals is a predictor of achievement. In Duckworth's theory, talent matters, but effort counts twice as grit breaks down to a formula:

talent x effort = skills

skills x effort = achievement.

Gritty people are familiar with applying extraordinary amounts of effort to achieve their goals. Thus, when they are faced with uncertainties or obstacles, they may be more capable of using the effort required to transform their situation into a positive outcome.[11]

Feeling Accomplished and Achieving Success. Applying one's strengths and achieving mastery in a specific domain is a key aspect of achieving the Good Life modeled through the PERMA Model of Well-being.[12] Grit is critical for any entrepreneur as they must maintain their unwavering motivation and commitment to achieve their desired level of success. By achieving their goals, they can increase their confidence and self-efficacy and improve their overall well-being.

A Key Contributor to Happiness and Life Satisfaction. Studies show that grit is associated with:

- happiness

- positive affect (exhibiting positive emotions like joy, gratitude, serenity, interest, hope, pride, amusement, inspiration, awe, and love)

- life satisfaction

As gritty entrepreneurs succeed in achieving their goals, they can feel a great source of accomplishment and satisfaction, igniting positive emotions and contributing to their overall happiness.[13]

CHAPTER FOUR

The Law of Entrepreneurial Connections: EntreConnections

THE STRENGTH OF YOUR RELATIONSHIPS OFTEN MIRRORS THE SUCCESS OF YOUR BUSINESS.

Human beings are born into this little span of life of which the best thing is its friendships and intimacies...and yet they leave their friendships and intimacies with no cultivation, to grow as they will by the roadside, expecting them to "keep" by force of mere inertia.

——William James

Since 2016, I have participated in LoToJa, a bike race of more than two hundred miles, over four mountain passes from Logan, Utah to Jackson Hole, Wyoming. It's the longest one-day sanctioned bicycle race in the United States, and it tests one's physical and mental stamina. I've finished the race four times and learned many life lessons along the road.

A couple of years ago, during a particularly brutal race, I realized the experience mirrored my entrepreneurial journey. Sometimes, the ride feels long. There are also many unexpected things that can happen. At times, you feel strong, confident, and able to pull others along. Other times, you hit a wall and need others to pull you.

In cycling, there is something called drafting. This is when a cyclist moves behind another cyclist's tire because it reduces wind resistance and the amount of energy required to pedal. Bike drafting saves about a third of your energy as you allow the person to pull you. When you gain energy, you can get out in front and start leading again.

There is a give-and-take that happens with drafting. You can't just drop behind someone else the entire ride. It feels a bit stingy. You have to reciprocate and force yourself to lead, so others can take advantage of the break.

During this race in 2021, I hit a mental wall at 110 miles in and at the top of the highest climb. I was exhausted and started throwing up. How was I going to finish the last 90 miles? The next forty-three miles were a blur as I jumped behind Brett, one of my riding buddies and hung on as best as I could.

When I reached the last leg of LoToJa—another forty-seven miles—I didn't know how much more I could give or if I'd be able to finish. Thankfully, my wife also bikes and was part of a relay team. She had already finished her race, so she accompanied me during those last forty-seven miles. For twenty miles, she got in front to help me conserve my energy, and then I was able to reciprocate the remaining twenty-seven miles, finishing forty-five minutes faster than my previous best time.

For the entrepreneur, there will be times when we lack energy or face a difficult climb. We need connections we can "draft" from. I believe those deeper positive connections in our lives have the same significant impact. We need people in our lives who can pull us through the inevitable ups and downs of entrepreneurship. Our ability to thrive depends upon it.

EntreConnections Help Us Persist

Just as your cycling success depends on drafting from others, for the entrepreneur, the Good Life starts with the people you surround yourself with. Our connections are central to our human need to belong.[72] We desire to be worthy of adding value and feeling valued.[73] In fact, lacking social connections and meaningful relationships can contribute to loneliness. Vice Admiral Vivek Murthy, MD, the US Surgeon General, has deemed loneliness an epidemic and a public health risk as studies indicate that loneliness surpasses the mortality risks of smoking fifteen cigarettes a day and obesity.[74] For this reason, it's a necessity for entrepreneurs to nurture connections, expanding relationships where they feel they can be authentically themselves.

Based on the longest standing research study on human connection, The Harvard Study of Adult Development, and then cited by authors and lead researchers Waldinger and Schulz in their recent book *The Good Life,* positive interactions with others help us feel safe by decreasing our physical and mental arousals.[75] They put us in a peaceful state and significantly contribute to our overall well-being. In contrast, negative interactions with others have the opposite effect, even to the point of producing stress hormones such as cortisol and adrenaline.

The Harvard Study of Adult Development, along with numerous others, show the most contributing factor to your well-being is your relationships, especially for entrepreneurs. As Waldinger and Schulz have noted, "the experience of having positive relations with others is a central feature of a positive, well-lived life."[76]

For entrepreneurs, connections are key to living the Good Life. According to a 2018 study, the timing of when an entrepreneur receives social support affects his ability to persist in his business:

Research finds that emotional support is most relevant earlier on during venture development, while instrumental support is most relevant for entrepreneurs who begin their businesses in earlier life stages.[77]

When I started my home-care business, I had never been an entrepreneur before. I also didn't have any background in home care, but I went for it. I was interested in business, so I took a chance.

Some of my closest relationships questioned my decision. They wondered if I'd be able to take care of my family. They wondered if I was taking too much of a risk. They questioned if I was ready for this.

Naysayers are those who don't believe in entrepreneurs or are concerned they are being rash. Often, these Negative Nellies are people who are close to us, so we hear their voices loud and clear. While these questions can come from a place of genuine concern, too many can be detrimental.

As an early entrepreneur, other people's doubts weighed on me. I needed someone to come alongside me and tell me they believed in me.

I needed to hear I could do it.

My wife and family, including both of our parents, were fortunately among those people who supported me, and I had someone else whose support was life-changing—my mentor Shane. Shane was a successful entrepreneur and mentor who helped me navigate the personal side of entrepreneurship. He helped me become a better person and head into my business venture for the right reasons.

Shane was also the one who loaned me the $15,000 I needed to keep my business afloat. His loan kept me going.

But Shane was more than just a mentor who loaned me money when I was in a desperate situation. He *believed* in what I was doing. I looked up to him and his success, so when he said, "You got this, Aaron. You can do this," it changed everything.

He was the high-quality connection (HQC) I needed. (More on HQC in the "run" section of this chapter.)

Shane didn't poke holes in my business plans. He didn't point out everything that was wrong. He supported me.

Research has shown the small-business mentoring experience is best facilitated when the mentor doesn't provide business advice or solutions to problems but helps the protégé explore ideas they can use to arrive at their own solutions.[78] This is what Shane did for me. Ultimately, entrepreneurs need people who believe in them regardless of whether they disagree with an idea or the direction you're going. If entrepreneurs can find those one or two key people who believe in them and can attach themselves early on, it can make all of the difference.

Surround yourself with positive people who encourage and believe in you. These are people who tell you, "You can do it!" or "You've got this!" You can continue on a difficult journey with the right people cheering you on. Both the giver and the receiver of such an interaction benefit. In psychology, we call this *capitalization*. This is a fancy word to describe that when someone responds in an active, constructive manner to someone else, both individuals experience positive emotions that combat loneliness and poor self-esteem. Capitalization is especially rewarding in intimate relationships, where it can deepen trust, closeness, and co mmitment.[79]

Here's a quick test to see if someone is truly on your side. Tell a friend some good news and gauge their response. As one study notes, an "enthusiastic and constructive response to a friend's good news is likely a disclosure of a deeper truth—an affirmation that they have their friend's best interest and goal pursuits in mind."[80] Surround yourself with these types of people who celebrate your success. Having others on your side will help you succeed.

One can read multiple pieces of literature about the importance of each of these different types of connections and their benefits to our overall well-being. However, as I studied these types of relationships, I discovered powerful characteristics required to truly cultivate them. I have personally found that these characteristics are consistent among entrepreneurs who are thriving and living their best lives. Though there are many characteristics that positively contribute to fostering deeper relationships, I will focus on three that I believe are vital for deeper connections for entrepreneurs.

EntreConnections CRAWL: The Congruent Entrepreneur

Of all the positive characteristics we are discussing in this chapter, congruence is certainly the one I struggle with the most. It does not come naturally for me and perhaps some of you can relate with that. Too often, I get caught up in presenting to the world, and even with closest relationships, a man who has it "all together." A kind father who never loses it with his kids, a selfless husband who always puts his wife first, and an entrepreneur who has the "golden touch" and only makes wise business decisions. To put it mildly, this is simply BS. I sometimes lose my cool with my kids, sometimes I put my own needs before my wife's, and trust me, I have made plenty of business mistakes, some of which have cost me millions, along with a wounded ego.

Several years ago, during the early stages of my first business venture, I left my car in a parking garage all day while attending an eight-hour training. I had pulled into the garage before business hours and was not aware of the cost to park there all day. As I left the garage and came to the exit gate, the attendant politely shared with me that I owed $45 for the day. As an early entrepreneur, she might as well have said $1,000, because I didn't have anything left in the bank account. I proceeded to uncharacteristically yell and blame the attendant for the issue, although it was entirely my fault for not reading the sign on my way in. After paying the $45, I left the garage feeling empty and immediately regretted the way

I had treated her for something that was clearly my fault, but I did not make the effort to go back and apologize. Internally, I justified my position and decided I wouldn't see her again anyway. I told myself it was fine. However, it was not fine. I had displayed a side of me that certainly was not congruent with who I believed and portrayed myself to be.

A few days later, we were attending our church and a new family had just moved into the area and was visiting for the first time. You guessed it. It was the parking garage attendant. In a city of over one million people, they just happened to attend my church only days after this incident. (The song, "Ironic," by singer Alanis Morisette is playing in my mind as I write this.)

She and her husband were already sitting when we walked in and immediately our eyes met. I quickly glanced away and pretended I did not see her. However, as I sat in my pew, I was overwhelmed with shame. How I had acted towards her was not how I wanted to be known. It was not who I wanted to be. This experience caused me to ask a lot of questions about who I was and how I wanted to live in private and in public. After our church meeting was over, I knew I needed to apologize and did. She kindly forgave me.

While covered more in EntreVigor and EntreAgency®, when these things happen, we must reframe them and let them go. If, in the past, we have acted in ways that are incongruent with who we really are, we must forgive (ourselves and ask for forgiveness from others), reframe, and move on. The day I asked for her forgiveness was a way to help realign my actions with who I portrayed myself to be. I was congruent once again. However, I could have easily lived incongruently and continued to portray myself as a great man publicly, while ripping people's heads off (metaphorically of course), in private. Unfortunately, there are some entrepreneurs who do just that. They are completely incongruent in their private and public relationships, stepping on people in private while presenting a positive nature in public on a regular basis.

Measured over weeks, months, years, and decades; I am not sure how some entrepreneurs survive this level of incongruence with their relationships.

So what does congruent mean to you? In 2008, David Stanley, a senior lecturer and researcher at University of Worcester, developed a new theory he entitled the "theory of congruent leadership." This theory was designed to describe the positive impact congruent clinical nursing leaders had on the people they cared for and supervised. David describes the congruent nurse leader's actions, activities, and deeds to match their own personal values, principles, and beliefs.[81] I love this definition and it certainly applies to us, the entrepreneurs. Congruence is when our actions, deeds, and activities align with our personal values, principles, and beliefs.

Go back to the Guiding Truths you created earlier. These truths should summarize what you value most in life. Do your choices, behaviors, interactions, private life, and everything you do align with your Guiding Truths? If so, you are a congruent entrepreneur. If you refer back to my own Guiding Truths, I can point out two areas right now that are incongruent. Not grossly so, but they are not aligned nonetheless. I am prone to incongruence like anyone else is. This is because we are all working towards congruence, at all times. The moment you think you've arrived should alarm you. You are likely deceiving yourself.

One area of my Guiding Truths involves relationships with my family. It states, "My family receives my time." When this is misaligned and incongruent, my Good Life looks more like "the selfish life," throwing my well-being on a downward spiral. I share this because it's an area that I have struggled with and I am confident the majority of entrepreneurs do as well. We can become addicted to our work and the adrenaline it provides us. For twenty years, I have loved my work overall. And I feel so blessed that I can confidently say this. But this addiction isn't always healthy and can negatively impact our family life. I have had to put guidelines in place, such as certain family traditions, to keep myself congruent with this portion of my Guiding Truths.

One family tradition, which focused on my time with my kids, started with my oldest child when he turned fourteen. The two of us took an epic ten-day trip together to Washington, DC, and several other American history sites. I have stayed true to this tradition with all six of my kids. This trip is usually one-on-one with dad or, if they desire, they can take another sibling with them. We have kept this fourteen-year-old trip within the United States and Mexico, seeing the Golden Gate Bridge, NFL® and MLB® games, Disney World®, Cancun, and lastly, of course, driving my friend's brand-new Porsche 911 with my youngest son. A ride he will never forget!

But the excursions don't stop once they hit fourteen.

When they become a senior in high school, we take another trip, and we go even bigger this time. So far, I've taken my seniors to Europe, Costa Rica, and the Virgin Islands...twice.

The point of these trips is to deepen my relationship with those closest to me. As a father and entrepreneur, I've found these trips extremely valuable. They have helped me thrive and grow. They have brought me closer to my children. They have created memories that will last a lifetime and be passed down for generations.

Most importantly, I am living out my Guiding Truths by staying congruent with the time I want to spend with my family. Traditions such as these help us stay on track with that purpose.

Before I conclude the crawl part of EntreConnections, I want to emphasize two key elements of congruence that as entrepreneurs, we must understand to truly thrive. I will introduce these elements in the form of two questions:

1. Are you comfortable being alone with your own thoughts, just being still and observing them? Or do you prefer to be entertained when you're alone by turning on NETFLIX, browsing the internet, and doing anything to keep from being alone in your own thoughts?

2. Who are the people in your life you spend time with that, when you're with them, create negative emotions, stress, and sometimes anxiety?

The first question is about you. If you are unable to sit with your own thoughts, which I have struggled with in the past, then you could be dealing with underlying incongruent parts of yourself. Something is misaligned. Shame is often the root cause of our inability to sit with our thoughts because it is easier to run from them. Dealing with shame requires self-awareness and self-acceptance. Practice sitting in your thoughts and let them flow. Find healthy ways to release the pain, anger, shame, and whatever else might be pushing you towards numbing your thoughts rather than being with them.

The second question is about the company you keep, your EntreConnections. Do you feel energy when you're around them? Do they allow you to be authentic in your personal and professional life? Are they self-accepting of who you are and what you hope to become? Congruence is far easier when we have people around us who inspire us to act and become who we say we are. The people we spend the most time with have a significant impact on our congruence and authenticity.

To assess your own congruence, go to **EntreThrive.com/Res ources** and take the *Congruent Entrepreneur Assessment*, designed to help bring awareness to your congruence and its alignment with your Guiding Truths.

EntreConnections WALK: The Present Entrepreneur

During my master's program at University of Pennsylvania, we were blessed with a lecture from Michael Baime, MD, who is the founder and director of the UPenn Program for Mindfulness, along with a clinical associate professor of medicine at the University of Penn School of Medicine. Dr. Baime's lecture was geared towards mindfulness and meditation practices that help us become more present with ourselves and others.

Shortly after his lecture, I read one of his recent papers for an assignment in the class, entitled, "Spiritual Transformation and

Health Through The Lifecycle." In this paper, Dr. Baime describes the typical doctor's office visit, where doctors have several patients to attend to and therefore have been programmed to cut to the chase, providing a diagnosis, recommendation, and follow-up. Though many doctors would like to be more present, the environment created in most doctor offices is not designed to foster it.

However, for one compassionate physician, Dr. Gowri Rocco, being present with her patients is central to providing the best care. She is known as the "Wellness Warrior" to her clients, who come from all over the world to work with her. She is also the author of *Growing Younger: Restore your Hormones, Energy, and Sex Drive.* I highly recommend reading it. Recently, I had the opportunity to sit down with Dr. Rocco and dig deeper into the topic of being present. Dr. Rocco's family came from an impoverished village in India, moving to America when she was six. Her father was an esteemed physician and so she decided to take a similar path. However, while doing her residency, she received the tragic news that her younger sister Padma, at the age of twenty-seven, took her own life. Ten years earlier, Padma was diagnosed with bipolar disorder and though she was receiving medical treatment during the time, the September 11, 2001, attacks on the World Trade Center triggered her mental illness (they lived close by at the time) and six days later, she was gone.

This tragedy was extremely difficult for Dr. Rocco and shook her faith in conventional medicine. Though she had considered leaving her residency, she stayed with it and has since made it her mission to focus her care on regenerative, anti-aging, spiritual wellness, and other kinds of preventative medicines. During the interview, she tenderly showed a picture of her sister and how she keeps it with her at all times, as a reminder to be all-in with her patients, because you really never know what they might be going through.

Dr. Rocco sees being present as the best way to help her patients begin the healing process. When she initially meets a new patient, she begins by asking them to name the three things they want to change with their health, rather than just focusing on the tests and diagnostics. She focuses on building trust immediately, knowing that she will also address the concerns brought up in the tests, but without that trust; they are less likely to listen.

To be present, she has to block out longer visits and set expectations that they might be waiting for her. In that sense, like other doctor offices, patients sometimes have periods of waiting. The difference is that they are just fine waiting! They know, that when it is their turn, they will have her undivided attention. She feels like she owes them her eye contact and genuine concern for their well-being.

Dr. Rocco also prays for every one of her patients, which helps her keep her focus on them and their needs, rather than thinking about the next patient. Dr. Rocco's unique approach to care has garnered national attention and given her the opportunity to provide care for well-known Hollywood stars, government officials, and the like. As a side note, during our interview, she practiced exactly what she shared with me. Though I was the interviewer, she was just as interested in finding out more about me and how I saw the world. In the "run" section of this chapter, we will talk about High-Quality Connections, which is exactly how I felt after our interview.

My point in sharing this story is to contrast that to the life of an entrepreneur. Put yourself in the place of most physicians. Like them, you have many who rely on you for direction, validation, love, guidance, advice, and the list goes on. It is easy for us, with all that we have to juggle, to treat our most important connections like a typical doctor's office. Your spouse might need your attention to make a decision on the landscaping, a child texts you with questions about how to handle a relationship, an employee comes into your office looking for advice on what to do about a difficult client, your business partner is asking for your help in mediating a challenging relationship he is having with another leadership team member, and the list goes on! How are you responding with each of these important connections? Are we fully present, like Dr. Rocco, or do we allow our mind to wander, thinking of the next problem that needs solving? Are you even listening to what they are saying? How do they feel when they interact with you and seek your help, support, and most importantly, your friendship? Are you truly present and sincerely interested in them?

As a historically distracted entrepreneur, being present with my most important connections has been a constant challenge and when I am not, my connections feel it. They sense I am not mentally present with them. Overtime, this erodes the connections vital to your well-being.

When I have been in entrepreneurial survival mode, stressed due to uncertainties and challenges at work, I can be prone to justifying letting some of my most important relationships receive less of my time, attention, and presence. I am guilty of telling myself, "Oh they will understand, they get me and why I have to do this." Can you relate with me?

Now, I understand that there are times when you have to be grinding to make your entrepreneurial dream a reality. The effort in writing this book is perhaps an example of this. However, I would argue that our attention and presence do not have to be sacrificed when our business demands more of our time.

What if we could take Dr. Rocco's being present approach with all of our closest personal and professional relationships? Even relationships that may not get a lot of our time but when we do connect with them, it's meaningful and real. They experience our attention and presence in a genuine, loving way. What impact would this kind of presence have on these relationships?

Here are a few evidence-based techniques that might help you become a more present entrepreneur:

- Time-blocking: Create self-discipline in your schedule by blocking time (physically blocking it out in your digital or paper calendar) where you are present and available for family, employees, customers, and other interactions. Making your most important relationships the priority. According to the *Academy of Management,*[82] setting aside blocks of time in your calendar can help increase focus. What better than to be focused and present with your most important relationships.

- Establishing boundaries: Using time-blocking, set your boundaries between personal and professional activities. Communicate these boundaries to your team members, so they understand when you're available. My team knows to never expect a reply in the evenings or weekends.

The *Journal of Occupational Health Psychology*[83] agreed and found that those who set boundaries between work and personal life reduce stress and improve well-being. It also provides the time to be present.

- Emptying space on your calendar: It is not always possible, but when you have a break between appointments, use that time to recharge and mentally prepare to be present for the next one.

- Active Listening: When you're in an important conversation, keep your attention on understanding what the other person is trying to express, while avoiding formulating your response while they are speaking. This is something my wife has mastered. According to an article in 2019 in the *International Journal of Listening*,[84] active listening leads to a deeper sense of wellbeing for leaders who practice it on a regular basis.

- Taking breaks, breaks, breaks: In the *Applied Psychology Journal*,[85] they cite that regular, short breaks during your day, especially during long tasks, can help improve your focus and attention. During the break, consider taking a moment to connect to your breath, connect to your five senses (what do you hear, see, feel, smell, and taste) and how do you feel somatically?

- Meditation to improve focus: Meditations, such as SKY (created by The Art of Living Center at ArtofLivingRetr eatCenter.org), help entrepreneurs become more aware of their thoughts and reactions to those thoughts. This helps improve engagement and active listening, as stated above. In a meta-analysis published in the 2012 *Psychological Bulletin*[86], meditation can help improve our physiology, attention, cognitive awareness, and positive emotions.

- Digital Fasting: Similar to time-blocking, set aside specific times to engage in social media, email, your phone messages, chats, etc. Technology is one of the greatest obstacles to being present with others. My team is well aware of my digital fasting and have learned that I do not respond right away to chats and other communications, especially when I am creating or trying to be present with my family. In the *Journal of Leisure Research*,[87] a study found that even the presence of a smartphone can reduce our cognitive abilities! Think on that one for a second.

- Practicing daily gratitude: Expressing gratitude to your most important relationships throughout the day, will help you improve well-being, reduce stress, and keep you grounded and present with them, according to the *Journal of Personality and Social Psychology*.[88]

- Adopting better sleep practices: Poor sleep will derail your ability to be present. This cannot be understated. If you struggle sleeping, get help! Find out the root cause and figure out how to overcome it. Deep and REM sleep is imperative to cognitive function and well-being, according to the Sleep Foundation's numerous studies.

  To be vulnerable, my dentist outfitted me with a "sleep appliance," that helps open up my airways at night and gives me a much better night's sleep. Find out what works for you!

- Ask for feedback: Finally and perhaps one of the most important, ask your relationships what you are doing well to be present and where you could use improvement. Ask them if there are times during the day/night that they wish you were more present with them. Actively listen to their feedback! Be present with it. If a deep level of trust exists, they will share and you will be all the better for it.

EntreConnections RUN: Amp Up Your High-Quality Connections

We all experience adversity in life, especially if you're an entrepreneur. This is why having resilience, the ability to adapt and carry on in the face of adverse conditions, is crucial. How do you build resilience?

Amp up your High-Quality Connections (HQCs).

According to research, social support, such as friendships, is essential to maintaining both physical and mental health.[89] The protective effect of good social support has been well documented. Here's the bottom line: if you have strong relationships, you're more likely to be resilient in the face of threats or challenges.

In addition to resilience, our connections can bring positivity and energy to our lives. Entrepreneurs have a unique opportunity to experience connection throughout the workday, sometimes with people they don't even know that well. However, we don't need to know a person well to have a "high-quality connection," or HQC. Dr. Jane Dutton coined the term, and according to Dutton, a "high-quality connection" is simply a *mutually beneficial* connection between two people.[90]

Dr. Dutton has a PHD in Organizational Psychology and, therefore, when she often refers to HQCs, it's in that context. However, many of the HQC principles apply to other types of relationships.

Several years ago, I was on a business trip and due to flight delays, arrived late in Boston, where I had to take a forty-five-minute Uber® ride to the hotel. My Uber driver was from Iran and immediately I could feel his positive energy as I took a seat in the back. Exhausted from my travels, I just wanted to close my eyes and rest, but I quickly found myself engaged in an interesting conversation with my driver. He expressed such interest in me, what I was doing, what I valued, and why I considered myself a spiritual person. It was a fascinating discussion between two men who had never met. It was an HQC.

As he pulled into the circular driveway of the hotel, he helped me with my bags and then gave me a huge bear hug and told me that he knew I would do great things. Wow! I was holding back the tears and walked away that night feeling deeply grateful for meeting this wonderful man. My entire week was better because of it. I am confident that if a research study were performed on the percentage of Uber drivers that hugged their passengers, it would be a fraction of a percent. This was a profound experience for me and continues to put a smile in my heart and on my face.

HQCs are all around us but especially accessible for those we are within arm's reach every day. For the entrepreneur, our homes and workplaces are full of HQC opportunities. These positive interactions enable both the individual and the collective at work to flourish and thrive. This is why we must connect with others—it not only affects us but our entire organization.

It is important to note that how we interact during a high-quality connection is just as important as making the effort. Dutton refers to this as *respectful engagement*. According to research, the way we talk, gesture, and even move our bodies during conversations; the quality of our connections is significantly enhanced.[91] The well-being benefits of HQCs are multiplied when we are present, engaged, and positioned to listen!

My Uber driver exemplified respectful engagement. Though he was sitting in front of me, he would slightly turn his head so I knew he was interested, while still ensuring our safety of course. He would get excited about certain experiences I shared and then repeat back sometimes how he interpreted them. He was actively listening and being present with me. He was amplifying our HQC, mind you, without a fancy degree in positive psychology! It came naturally to him. Same goes for Dr. Rocco when she interacts with her patients. She has mastered respectful engagement.

HQCs for entrepreneurs feed our souls and the souls of those we interact with, even when we think we are too busy to connect with our teams. In one of my previous successful ventures, my former business partner, Erik Madsen, was the master at high-quality connections.

One day at work, I saw Erik sitting down with one of our research associates he didn't know well. I overheard Erik asking about the person's life, asking about any frustrations he had, and asking how he could better serve this associate. The individual was extremely connected to the conversation, and so was Erik.

Witnessing their interaction changed me as a leader.

I was amazed to see how much time Erik spent connecting with one person. I was even more amazed to learn he got so much out of those conversations as well. In fact, those conversations energized him. Both he and his connection benefitted from the interaction. It was a high-quality connection because he practiced respectful engagement. He was present.

Another behavior important to HQCs is what Dutton refers to as *task enabling*. This is when our goal in the HQC is to help first, especially when it comes to those we employ. If we approach HQCs in a genuine effort to help the other person, the overall commitment to the relationship grows for both parties and improves productivity in a team environment.

How often are you having high-quality connections at work? Studies suggest that even small amounts of interaction can "improve both persons' cognitive performance in terms of speed of processing and working memory performance."[92] The impact of such a connection is undeniable. It is especially impactful when you, the entrepreneur, their boss, takes a sincere interest in them.

For entrepreneurs, we have the opportunity for this kind of consistent high-quality connection every day. We have the ability to energize our workplace through our connections. In the introduction of this book, I expressed my sincere desire to help you create the Good Life, in the hopes you would spread it to your team. HQCs are foundational to the spreading of the Good Life to others.

EntreConnections FLY: Level Up Your Relationships

When it comes to creating the Good Life for ourselves, nothing gets us there faster than deepening our most important relationships. However, to do so, you must be willing to step into relationships that, at first, might intimidate you and create some healthy discomfort.

Recently, I made the financial and time investments to join an elite group of high-level entrepreneurs (collectively worth in the billions), to increase my learning, confidence, and most importantly, collaborate with some of the smartest minds in business. This has not been the most comfortable 10x jump for me. Imposter syndrome and the feeling I was in over my head has certainly creeped into my narrative. However, I put on my big-boy pants and showed up to my first meeting with this group prepared to contribute in any way I could.

For every breakout, discussion, and opportunity to connect, I was present and took interest in each and every one. I quickly realized these women and men were regular people, like me, who are just trying to make a bigger difference in the world. Our whys are aligned. That was one of the best full-day collaboration sessions of my career. I had several HQCs and felt my congruent nature lent itself to others in the group. I spoke with a few of my fellow members and they felt the same as I did, that I was walking out of that room a better person, leader, entrepreneur, and friend. Because I had "leveled up" my relationship by joining this special group of entrepreneurs, my ability to flourish and thrive has also leveled up.

Where can you level up your relationships? Both with your existing most important relationships but also ones that currently do not exist. Are there mentors you wish you had, personal relationships that need more of your presence? Business groups that will level up your thinking and opportunities? Write them down. Make a plan to connect deeper with your important existing relationships, the ones that give you energy. Then, make a plan to forge new relationships that will take you to new levels of growth, awareness, and well-being!

As a side note, also mentioned in EntreClarity, list the relationships that create negative emotions and are keeping you from leveling up with new ones. We all have them. Relationships that drain our energy and people who are jealous when you try to grow beyond where they are at. They hold you back from leveling up and keep you from creating the Good Life.

A word of caution here, be wise when it comes to family. I do believe there are some family relationships that you must separate yourself from due to toxicity and overall damage to your well-being. Get out of those toxic relationships so you can flourish personally. However, there are times when a family member might need more of your love, presence, and respectful engagement! Maybe they need your best self to show up for them and then reciprocation of the relationship can take root and blossom over time. Be mindful of the difference between a toxic relationship and one that deserves more of your time, attention, and love. I have been guilty of distancing myself from relationships that simply needed my attention in order to grow.

Let's be clear. EntreConnections is not only about hitching your wagon to the right people but also learning how to be the right person for others. In fact, I would argue this is even more important. To do this, consider (1) your congruence and if it is aligned with who you are, (2) if you're truly mindful and present with your family, team members, customers, and friends, and (3) if you are truly experiencing high-quality connections daily.

As a reminder, the Law of EntreConnections states, "*The strength of your relationships often mirrors the success of your business.*" Congruence, presence, and HQCs are all ways to strengthen and deepen those relationships you care about the most. By doing so, your business stands to benefit in significant and profound ways.

Next Actions

- Take the *Congruent Entrepreneur Assessment* at **EntreT hrive.com/Resources.**

Focus on a couple of areas where you can create greater alignment in your life. Incongruence gets in the way of being present and having HQCs.

- Using your goals of being more present and congruent, strive to create at least one HQC every day. Practice respectful engagement and task enabling. Be intentional in each HQC and you'll find deeper happiness.

- Join a community of entrepreneurs that will help you level up. At EntreThrive, we are building such a community, focused on helping entrepreneurs learn how to adopt the Good Life mindset, where they can flourish personally and professionally. To learn more and join this meaningful community of like-minded entrepreneurs, go to **EntreThrive.com**.

EntreConnections help us create the Good Life, perhaps more than any other. However, the next law, EntreFaith, is not far behind in its importance and potential impact. That is the next law of EntreThrive.

The Science Behind the Law of EntreConnections and How It Can Help You to Create Your Good Life

Physical Health and Longevity. Forming healthy relationships is essential to our well-being. As human beings, we are wired and motivated to form social bonds. We have what psychologists theorize is a *need to belong*.[22] Social connection is a health determinant. A study revealed that among all major causes of death, mortality rates were higher among people who lacked social bonds than for people who were well-connected to other people.[15]

Happiness and Greater Quality of Life. Sharing your interests, hobbies, work, and life experiences with family, friends, and a community enriches your life and makes it more joyful, fulfilling, and purposeful. Research shows that happy people are social and have stronger romantic and other social relationships than less happy people.[23]

Mental Health and Resilience. Having strong social connections can nurture our resilience and be a protective factor on our mental health. Our relationships are forms of social support that can help buffer the stress and anxiety that accompany life challenges we encounter. They can help us to bounce back from adversity. In fact, the importance of social relationships is so important to our well-being, that it is a core component of teaching soldiers to strengthen their social relationships in a Master Resilience Training program in the U.S. Army.[24]

Self-Esteem and Identity. Being part of a group and community contributes to our sense of belonging and can help us to feel more valued. These feelings can validate our identity, reinforce a positive self-image, and foster greater feelings of self-worth and self-esteem. Research shows that our sense of mattering, whereby we feel valued and add value, is linked to our well-being. Mattering helps us to feel empowered and can be catalysts to building resilient communities.[25]

CHAPTER FIVE

The Law of Entrepreneurial Faith: EntreFaith

YOUR FUTURE IS BRIGHTER THAN WHAT YOU CAN SEE AND FEEL.

Faithless is he that says farewell when the road darkens.
—J.R.R. Tolkien

Soon after we moved to Idaho in 2007, I began to dream of living along the famous Snake River, which runs through our community. As someone who loves the outdoors and fishing, river life was practically designed for me. I shared this dream with my wife and it quickly turned into a shared dream for both of us. However, buildable and convenient property on the Snake River is extremely difficult to find. Plus, at the time, we couldn't afford such a property! But deep down, I believed that living on the river symbolized a personal breakaway that could provide lasting positive memories for our family for decades to come and I refused to stop looking.

My dream wasn't a small one. At the time, I was running an innovative, growing company and experiencing growing pains with that new exponential growth. Juggling my personal and professional responsibilities with this new dream required the EntreGrit I described earlier.

After several years of searching, one day my wife and I were looking over aerial views of our county and our eyes caught hold of a special property. You could say it was love at first sight. The land consisted of twenty-three acres with a home from the 1950s on a perfect building spot connected to and overlooking the beautiful Snake River.

Unfortunately, the property wasn't for sale, but we began pursuing it anyway. Grasping for any information we could get and just when I was about to approach the owners, a realtor friend of ours listed it on their behalf. I couldn't believe it! Just like that, our dream property was up for sale. However, our excitement turned to reality quickly. The property was ready for us, but it was too soon, we weren't ready for it. I had recently invested a significant amount of our personal capital back into our growing business. Therefore, we lacked the cash necessary to compete against future offers.

So, my wife and I prayed about it. We felt a yearning deep within for a property such as this. It was going to be our home. This was the life I'd envisioned all of those years ago.

I wasn't alone in thinking it was the perfect property, as others lined up to purchase it too. At one point, the property had three different offers that somehow all fell through due to financing. Though they were asking a fair price, due to the lack of comparable inventory in the area, loan appraisals were coming up short. They needed a cash buyer, and so, this property sat on the market longer than anyone thought it would. Then, it happened.

Unexpectedly, another investor in our industry approached me and wanted to buy a few shares of my company. Because it was good for our company and its future, we moved forward with the deal, and suddenly, I had the cash available to purchase the property. Our prayers had been answered. We made a cash offer closer to the recently appraised value and gratefully the owners accepted.

In time, the land on the banks of the Snake River—our dream property—became ours against all odds.

This big dream required faith. It required us to believe it could happen, even when we had no idea how the pieces would come together. It required us to believe that God cared about our big dreams, too, and would make a way for us, even when the road was bumpy and ridden with potholes. As the pieces slowly fell into place, we knew we had been blessed.

Though building our dream home on the property turned out to be quite the trial of our faith, our grit and resolve to push through it was often fueled by the knowledge that the property came to us because of our faith in ourselves, others, and God.

Today, as I sit on my property and gaze out the window at the breathtaking view, which, by the way, includes a visual of our newfound friend, a moose we have affectionately named Waldo, I am reminded of the miracles that ensued once we moved forward with our vision in faith.

EntreFaith Solves Your Greatest Entrepreneurial Hurdles

For entrepreneurs who love to create, build, and dream, sometimes we can struggle with taking the first step. Stepping out in faith that we can make an idea happen can also drum up a host of doubts and second guessing. However, in the words of Dieter F. Uchtdorf, a renowned airline pilot and now spiritual leader, "First, doubt your doubts before you doubt your faith."[97]

Faith is not just for the religious and/or spiritual. Regardless of your beliefs, faith is a term that should be woven throughout the entrepreneurial experience. As an entrepreneur, stepping into the unknown, taking the leap, per se, requires a deeper commitment and willingness to accept the uncertainties that come. Hence, the reason we call it EntreFaith—because it requires you to embrace the unknown, which you can neither see nor feel as an entrepreneur.

Dr. Martin Luther King, Jr. once said, "Faith is taking the first step even when you do not see the whole staircase."[98]

Faith allows us to accept change and leave behind those things that don't support our "breakaways." As Dr. Henry Cloud wrote in his book *Necessary Endings*,

Being alive requires that we sometimes kill off things in which we were once invested, uproot what we previously nurtured, and tear down what we built for an earlier time.[99]

For entrepreneurs to grow and become their better, future selves, we must change and "kill off" that which holds us back.

However, to "kill off" requires us to move forward in faith—not fear.

Because EntreFaith helps us believe our future is brighter than what we can see or feel, it helps us deal with and accept uncertainty. Entrepreneurs will inevitably face uncertainties in life and in business, but if we believe there is something greater in store for us, we can push through, even when our vision dims. Tough times will not be the reason we give up. They will cause us to cling to our hope in a bigger, better future.

No big goal has ever been achieved without some kind of faith—faith in ourselves, faith in others, or faith in a higher power. Often, faith encompasses all three. If we desire to be courageous individuals who take on seemingly impossible challenges, we must have faith.

EntreFaith CRAWL: Faith In Yourself

The EntreFaith journey begins with faith in oneself. That is, you believe you have what it takes to make something happen. While you may not always know *how* you are going to achieve something or perhaps the way is not yet clear, you still believe you'll be able to figure it out.

In positive psychology, faith in one's abilities to figure things out is called self-efficacy. Self-efficacy, a term coined by renowned psychologist Albert Bandura, is a person's belief they have the skills and abilities to produce a positive outcome.[100] If we have self-efficacy, we believe we can succeed, and Bandura believes this faith in ourselves is one of the most powerful predictors of performance and well-being. We dive even deeper into the powerful concept of self-efficacy in the last law, EntreAgency.

As entrepreneurs, we're inevitably going to experience hardships and encounter unexpected troubles. We most likely will have no idea how to solve many of these issues the first time around. For the entrepreneur to truly flourish, we must have the confidence to say to ourselves, "I can figure this out." We must truly believe everything is figure-out-able, which includes identifying resources, people, etc. that can help you figure it out. This belief in ourselves will stop us from experiencing too many sleepless nights and fear-filled days freaking out about the unknown. This uncharted territory will simply be a problem to solve instead of a problem that destroys.

When I undertook the home-care industry's first benchmarking study, I needed faith in myself. Math was not something that came to me naturally, and I routinely found myself earning Cs in high school math. Not only that, but I lacked a statistical background entirely. But I still believed I could learn how to do it. Belief is the key to thriving. I had faith in myself, which enabled me to step into the unknown. Success rests on your determination and ability to work with what you have and figure the rest out.

For my first-ever benchmarking study, I lacked the financial means and the overall vision of what the study needed to look like. I didn't know how to hire what Dan Sullivan calls the right who to hand the project over to. But somewhere deep down within, I truly believed I could do it, so I refused to give up. I had a vision of what the industry needed, and I believed I could create something the industry had never seen before. People in the industry were hungry for the kind of data and information my study could provide.

Currently, this study is the largest and most respected study for the entire home-care industry and has been published every year since 2010. It's like the Bible for the home-care industry—home-care entrepreneurs rely on it to help them scale and grow their businesses. This massive undertaking came about simply because I had faith in my abilities to figure it out.

But the journey wasn't without its ups and downs. I dealt with the usual self-doubt and the desire to give up reared its ugly head again and again. There were times I felt so discouraged that it brought me to tears—even up to the moment I was sleeping under my desk. However, these are the moments where we must dig deep and remind ourselves of our purpose, trusting our grit can sustain us until our faith in a positive outcome fully kicks in.

Our Story vs. Our Narrative

"Our story" consists of the actual events that have taken place in our lives. "Our narrative," on the other hand, is the story we tell ourselves about our lives. For example, if you take on a venture that fails, that is what happened. It's part of your story. But what narrative do you tell yourself about that failed venture? Do you call yourself a risk-taker? Is it a tale of adventure and learning? Or do you simply see it as a story of failure—or more significantly of *your* failure?

Pay attention to the narrative you tell yourself because our narrative is part of our identity. Faith in yourself may sometimes require you to tell yourself a narrative that isn't true *today* but is what you want to be true about yourself *tomorrow*. However, going back to EntreClarity and identity, your narrative must also be accompanied with massive action, otherwise it can turn into a *false narrative*, which can negatively impact our happiness.

The Faith to Let Go

Sometimes, to grow in faith in ourselves, we have a breakaway that requires us to let go of the past or other things that no longer serve us. Dr. Henry Cloud, in *Necessary Endings*, calls this faith process "pruning," and he explains the three types of situations where pruning may be required:[101]

1. If a former activity or initiative pulls resources that should go towards your Breakaway, prune it.

2. If something in your personal or professional life no longer serves your future desired self, prune it. (This could even include relationships.)

3. If something is dead but we struggle to let go of it because of fear, guilt, or some other emotion, prune it.

For our breakaways to be possible, pruning is necessary. For example, when I created my Breakaway benchmark study, my life was full of both personal and professional pruning. I had to let go of initiatives that would not support my breakaway. I also had several ineffective activities that ate away at my time and attention and distracted me from my breakaway—they had to go.

Pruning, however, can be a difficult process. It requires faith in yourself to let go and become the person you desire to be. You must believe you have it within you to become your future, better self.

As we prune away that which won't help us grow, we shouldn't shamefully discard our "former self." Instead, show gratitude for your former self, as someone who grew from what they learned. You're someone who opened new doors, learned from challenges, failed, and decided to get back up again.

Pruning also means recognizing those in our lives who want us to stay the way we were—people who keep their own frame of our past and believe it is still true about us today.

Thirty years ago, I returned home from a two-year mission for my church, and it was transformational. I left a complacent life behind and grew leaps and bounds during this period. When I returned, my older brother Bryant gave wise advice that has forever stayed with me. He said, "Many people who knew you before you left will forget you've changed for the better and will try and treat you as if you never left. If you believe this lie, you will end up falling back into old patterns of complacency and bad habits." He couldn't have been more right. People, as well as ourselves, are guilty of framing our past in certain ways and then applying that frame to present and future events. Several friends tried to pretend nothing had changed and wanted things to remain the way they were before. I had pruning to do after my mission, which included distancing myself from relationships that treated me like nothing had changed. Though difficult at times, listening to my brother's advice opened up the opportunities for me to become an entrepreneur five years later.

In the end, EntreFaith begins with believing in yourself. While this certainly means we believe everything is "figure-out-able," it also means we believe we are *worthy* of what we want and desire. We shouldn't apologize for what we want. We need to believe we belong, we matter, and what we want also matters. This kind of EntreFaith is key to thriving.

EntreFaith WALK: The Courage to Put Your Faith in Others

Take a moment to think of someone in the past you looked up to and trusted you with something. This person believed you had what it took to figure out a solution. This individual put his or her faith in *you*.

- How did this experience make you feel? Write down the positive emotions you experienced, such as love, gratitude, etc.

- How did this individual's faith increase your faith in yourself?

Dale Green was a financial advisor, a highly successful entrepreneur, and most importantly, one of my closest friends. Dale is one of those people whose faith in me changed my faith in myself. Interestingly, Dale's faith in me occurred at one of the most stressful points in my entrepreneurial journey.

At the time my company was growing, our billables hadn't quite caught up with our many expenses. As a result, we needed cash—quickly. By that point, I'd already invested hundreds of thousands of my own money, and I didn't have any more cash to invest. Sensing the desperate situation, my wife and I began to pray for a solution.

I also began talking to people about investing in my company, but I never asked Dale. Because he was such a good friend of mine, I didn't feel comfortable approaching him in that manner. However, during one of our many lunches, Dale shared he had considerable Apple® stock to sell and wondered if I was looking for an investor. He, unlike me, had cash handy and was looking for a place to put it.

His words were an answer to prayer.

I revealed the truth to him—my company was growing but we needed an investor. Dale willingly put his trust and his resources before me. He revealed he couldn't imagine trusting anyone more than me. I was beyond grateful for the support.

Dale's generosity changed not only my business but also my life. His faith in me propelled my faith in myself. My self-confidence grew a little more that day. Someone I greatly respected and admired believed in me, trusted me. I now had one more reason to believe and trust in myself. His faith in me grew into my own faith in me.

On April 22, 2022, Dale passed away after a two-year battle with cancer. His passing was one of the hardest deaths I've ever experienced, and I will forever be grateful for him—for the kind of person he was, for the kind of friend he was, and for the way his faith in me changed the course of my own life.

- Who in your life, personal and professional, has *earned* your faith in them? Write down their names. How can you be their Dale? Not necessarily in a financial way but demonstrating your faith in them. Take action on this list and you'll find that by putting your faith in others, your well-being will be nourished.

Over the years, I've put my faith in many people. The experience has been beneficial for those on the receiving end and for me as well. These individuals, also known as my "Whos," make my life better. They help me to thrive because I know I have people who I can count on.

Trust Begets Trust

One of the greatest myths is that our faith and trust in others are *earned* first. I don't believe this. I believe this is unhealthy. While we certainly must discern the trustworthiness of others, especially early on in the relationship, we shouldn't wait for people to earn our trust. Instead, we should trust our first impressions, our gut, our spiritual discernment, how we are about a person, and if their core values align with our own. After we gauge their trustworthiness (or lack thereof), we can then begin to either place (or withhold) our faith in them.

When we wait for people to earn our trust, we fail to share with them how we "keep score."[102] In this situation, nobody knows how to win because they aren't trusted with anything. On the other hand, if we recognize trust as the responsibility of the other person, then we can freely give it. This means we can trust others with tasks and challenges, and if they want to be trusted, it's their responsibility to fulfill their end of the bargain. If they do well, they reveal themselves to be high-trust individuals.

As Mike Robbins says, trust is something we *grant* to others—we don't require them to earn it.[103] It's ultimately up to us to grant others our trust (or not) and then continue to trust them (or not). By granting our trust to others, we create healthy families, teams, organizations, and communities. Trusting allows us to grow and flourish, whereas a lack of trust creates a stressful, hostile, and damaging environment.

It is good to give our trust to others, but it is best for trust to be reciprocated. As Mahatma Gandhi said, "Trust begets trust. Suspicion is fetid and only stinks. He who trusts has never yet lost in the world."[104] When we willingly give our trust to others, their trust is almost always returned to us. Trust tends to create more trust.

When we have faith in others, we are truly trusting the good in humanity. Trusting others also allows us to step beyond ourselves and not merely rely on our own abilities. It helps us to see beyond ourselves by finding those we can put our faith in.

Successful leaders have always recognized the importance of granting your faith to others. As Jim Collins said, "Leaders of great companies first ask who, then what."[105] Stephen M. R. Covey writes in *Trust and Inspire* that "our most significant challenge is not a lack of trustworthy people—the biggest challenge is trustworthy people who do not extend trust to other trustworthy peo ple."[106] In addition, one of the core teachings of EOS Worldwide®, the leading entrepreneurial business system I have used in my own businesses, is the concept of "Right People, Right Seats."[107]

Last year I hired a new full-time strategic assistant to help assist me with all of our holdings. Because of my faith in myself to hire based upon our core values and what EOS Worldwide calls Get It, Want It, and Capacity To Do it (GWC), I hired this new assistant with confidence. Within the first week, she had access to confidential information, including passwords. She was pleasantly surprised by my immediate trust in her, which has cultivated a very positive working relationship ever since.

If we hire the right people, then they are trustworthy. We need to put our faith in them and in their ability to help us grow. You simply provide them the opportunity to rise to the occasion. Will you sometimes get burned? Yes, and if you do, evaluate why. Great leaders ask, "Was it I?" before pointing any fingers at the other party. Sometimes, we do a poor job of hiring the right people and therefore blame them, when in reality, you just didn't hire them based upon your "right people" criteria.

EntreFaith RUN: Faith in the Transcendent

Dating back to 1998, the World Health Organization presented findings that spiritual health was directly related to our physical health. This was backed by another study conducted by an entire team of researchers just a few years later.[108] Spiritual health can, of course, incorporate various types of relationships, even outside of God or a belief in a higher power.

A highly respected study conducted to assess the impact four types of spiritual relationships have on our well-being was conducted via a questionnaire entitled Spiritual Health and Life-Orientation Measure (SHALOM). SHALOM measured the relationships with self, others, the environment, and what they referred to as the Transcendent (God, higher-power, spiritual beings, etc.). What they found was that the highest contributing factor to spiritual well-being, among the four domains, was the relationship we have with the Transcendent. It is important to note that the other three domains still have a positive impact on spiritual well-being, especially when they are connected to one or more of the other domains. For example, our relationships with others can influence our relationships with the environment, God, and self.

Turning to another body of research conducted by Kauanui et. al. grouped entrepreneurs into two groups—"cash is king" and "make me whole."[109] Cash is king entrepreneurs defined success in terms of reaching financial goals. Their eyes were on the financial prize. Those in the make me whole group, sought meaning and purpose in their lives and believed their work could impact, inspire, and change others for the better. Not surprisingly, those who sought purpose and were spiritually oriented (Make me Whole entrepreneurs) had a heightened sense of joy in both their work and life.

Other studies have shown spirituality has a positive effect on entrepreneurial pursuits. For the spiritually inclined, they reported higher life satisfaction, higher sales, hiring, and productivity growth rates, and reduced stress. As one researcher put it, "No organization can survive long without spirituality and soul."[110]

Spirituality can also shape our values and how we ethically behave in business. When faith drives our actions, virtues tend to manifest themselves more, which translates into a better work en vironment.[111] Entrepreneurs with strong faith in a higher power often see their businesses as a platform to serve others and make a bigger impact in their communities. Their faith leads to impact.

My goal is to try and convince you how a belief in the Transcendent, God, or a high-power, is directly correlated to creating the Good Life. If you find yourself raising an eyebrow to my point here, I challenge you to do your own research and deep dive into the topic and come to your own conclusion. I just ask you to keep an open mind to what you discover. Wherever you are with your faith in a Transcendent being, you will find no judgment here and what I share comes from a place of sincere gratitude that you're willing to hear me out on this important topic.

Faith in the Impossible

Part of EntreFaith is developing faith in God, the Transcendent, a higher spiritual power, or whatever term resonates with your current beliefs, which can help the impossible become possible. I will use the term "God," as that resonates most with me, but please, feel free to insert whatever term helps you find a deeper meaning from a power greater than self.

We believe this power can make up for what we lack and make a way for us. This concept is illustrated by religious leader Stephen E. Robinson's "The Parable of the Bicycle."[112] In this parable, a little girl desperately wants a bike. Unfortunately, she doesn't have the money to purchase one, so her father tells her to save up all of her pennies and eventually she'll have enough. While the girl saves and saves her pennies and takes on extra chores to earn money, she ends up with only sixty-one cents. She knows this isn't enough for a bike and begins to worry she'll never have enough. But her father steps in, and in exchange for her sixty-one cents, plus a hug and a kiss, he agrees to buy her a bike. Her impossible dream was made a reality by her loving father.

This story illustrates how we all desire something desperately, yet no matter how hard we try, we tend to come up short. For the Christian, we fall short of the glory of God and Heaven, but God makes a way for us through Christ and His atonement. Whether a Christian or not, none of us have everything we need to accomplish all we desire. We all need a miracle now and then. We all need help that comes from outside of ourselves. We could apply this same parable to most things in life, where we often can accomplish far more with the right whos.

While we certainly need to bring to the table all of our skills, strategies, abilities, and all of the right whos, in the end, for me, God has been the most important Who in my life. I attribute God to helping me and my family cross those impossible finish lines. He can make miracles happen. The Bible speaks of God's ability to fill in the gap between what's impossible and possible in Matthew 19:26 (King James Version): "But Jesus beheld them, and said unto them, With man this is impossible; but with God all things are possible.'"

As mentioned earlier, when my business was quickly running out of cash, we needed a miracle, so I began to pray. But my faith didn't stop there. I also sought help from other people, looked for solutions, and did everything in my power to keep my business going. I didn't just sit on my hands and wait around for God to work out a miracle. While I believe God can certainly perform a miracle based on a person's prayer alone, faith often requires us to *act* on our faith. This means we trust God to move, and our faith propels us to move as well. We put forth our best effort *because* we have faith.

Faith in God also requires faith in the actual outcomes. Sometimes what we want and what God wants may differ. If the outcome is different than what we hoped for, we have to trust God's plan for our lives. His ways are different from our ways. His plans are greater than our own, and faith in God means trusting His plan more than your own. When we truly trust God with the outcome, peace often outweighs the frustration and fear.

Time and again, I find myself facing the feelings of inadequacy that comes with stepping foot into the void of the unknown. Likewise, time and again, I find myself crossing finish lines I felt were impossible to cross. I crawled, I walked, I ran, I flew, and I attribute these successes to my relationship with God. While I know my skills and relationships with others certainly help, God ultimately makes my dreams a reality. With faith in my abilities and faith in the right whos, God has made up the difference, just like the father did with his daughter and the bicycle. Our impossible breakaways become possible with God in our corner.

Saying this, the next section outlines the imperfect faith in a higher power we often have to start with.

A Faith Hurdle Can Lead to Flourishing

While EntreFaith is essential, it's not effortless. Though we believe God is perfect, we also know our faith is not. Our faith ebbs and flows. It can even wane depending on our life circumstances. When life hits us hard, our faith can falter.

I experienced my own faith hurdle a few years ago when one of my children dealt with an extremely challenging situation. Nothing about it felt fair. This struggle wasn't something my child had asked for nor was it the result of any bad choices. As a father, I questioned God's plan and purpose in the reality we faced. I love my kids, and I know God does too. Even still, I wondered if God listened to my pleas for help. Did He really care?

At the time, I oversaw the spiritual health of approximately 140 individuals as a young adult minister at our local university. Yet, even as someone who led others in their faith, my faith was being severely challenged. Referring back to EntreConnections, I was in a state of incongruence relative to my faith, one of my core Guiding Truths.

Through the experience, I learned that often life's difficulties force us to dig deeper into our faith. They compel us to ask difficult questions about God and our existence. Do we still believe God is good, even when everything appears to be in shambles? When our faith is tested, it has the potential to come out on the other side purified and stronger.

Over the years, I've discovered EntreFaith—whether it's our faith in God, in others, or in ourselves—requires effort. Letting go is tough as an entrepreneur. I want to control the narrative and the outcomes. However, that isn't how this life works. By letting go and giving some of my burdens to God, this frees me to focus on what I can control and what others can help me control. For me, the Good Life is more complete when I have allowed God inside it.

If your faith in a higher power is something you are struggling with, you're not alone. Many of us have been there. Start small by first planting the seed. And with any seed, it's best to find fertile ground, so it has the best chances of growth. Going back to Entre-Connections, if growing your faith in a higher power is important to you, surround yourself with people who can help you plant the seed. This outreach involves a variety of methods, including the possibility of finding a religious and/or spiritual group that you trust. In fact, a research team led by respected psychologist David Yaden, found that those who had a religious affiliation tend to have a higher sense of well-being, live longer, and overall experience better health.[113]

Surrounding myself with people of faith extends beyond my own religious affiliation as a Christian. I have rubbed shoulders with people of faith who are Hindu, Muslim, Buddhist, and those who are simply spiritual in nature. All these individuals have had a profound positive impact on my life and on my faith. The key is to put your trust in those that align with your own journey of faith.

EntreFaith FLY: Faith to Give Freely (Time, Money, Energy)

EntreFaith—believing in yourself, in others, and in something bigger than yourself—is essential to entrepreneurs.

EntreFaith means you don't have to do it all on your own. We bring this to our work and experience greater joy. We also benefit by not having to bear the weight of the world on our shoulders.

Once we have developed our EntreFaith crawl, walk, and run, we can begin to fly. Here our faith enables us to freely give and serve others. We can give of our time, our resources, and our energy.

For many entrepreneurs, their purpose is to serve others. They desire to make the world a better place. As we grow in our Entre-Faith, we become more and more willing to follow our purpose and serve others. By doing so, our joy and life satisfaction continues to increase, as the true blessing comes when we give, not when we receive.

Next Actions

1. Complete another Breakaway tool (**EntreThrive.com/ Resources**) and this time focus your breakaway on an activity that will strengthen your faith in yourself, others, or God. Go all in on this breakaway! Prune those things that will hold this breakaway back.

2. Find ways to put your faith in action, by giving your trust early on in a new relationship, whether personal or professional.

3. Based upon your own faith journey, evaluate your faith in the Transcendent, God, a higher power. What can you do to strengthen this faith or at least plant the seed? Write out one step you want to take in this area.

The Science Behind the Law of EntreFaith and How It Can Help You to Create Your Good Life

Faith and spirituality can provide a framework to elicit greater hope and optimism, which according to studies is associated with life satisfaction, greater mental health, lower levels of depression and anxiety. Researchers Petersen and Seligman share that when individuals activate their character strengths of hope and optimism, they elevate their psychological well-being and happiness.[18]

Spirituality and religion are associated with life sati sfaction.[19] One way that religion and spirituality can impact life satisfaction is by enhancing positive affect (positive emotions like gratitude, serenity, hope, awe, and love).

Trust is strongly associated with life satisfaction and well-being. Studies showed an 18 percent increase in life satisfaction among people who had high levels of trust across all domains; their co-workers, neighbors, and the police.[20]

Religious affiliation correlates to individuals having a higher sense of well-being, living longer, and overall, experiencing better health.[21]

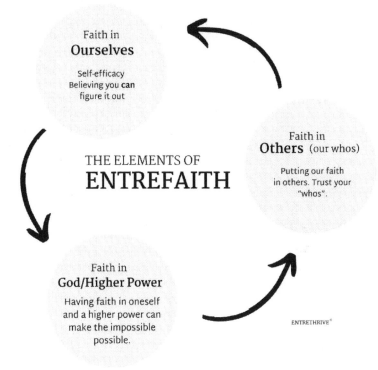

After discussing the various ways in which EntreFaith allows us to succeed, to flourish, and to make our wildest dreams a reality, we'll examine the Law of EntreHabits—the daily habits to implement that will help us thrive and create the Good Life.

CHAPTER SIX

The Law of Entrepreneurial Habits: EntreHabits

ULTIMATE PERFORMANCE FLOWS FROM YOUR UNCONSCIOUS CHOICES.

Habits work for us in ways that our conscious decisions never can.

—Wendy Wood

When we think about our daily habits, we typically conjure up ideas about waking up early, reading more books, taking our daily supplements, and getting our morning exercise in. However, there is more to daily habits than improving our health or fulfilling our to-do lists. We can also use our habits to cultivate and grow our character strengths. And sometimes, our habits can help us achieve the seemingly impossible.

"This is far and away the most dangerous thing we've ever attempted."[118] Tom Cruise spoke these words about his stunt in *Mission Impossible: Dead Reckoning Part 1*. In the film, Cruise would perform a stunt that required him to ride a motorcycle off an enormous cliff in Norway. As those involved in the risky ordeal noted, they were trying to avoid two things: severe injury and death.

To prepare for such a dangerous stunt, Cruise trained tirelessly. He took five hundred skydive base jumps and thirteen thousand practice motocross jumps to prepare both his mind and body. Cruise consciously worked on these jumps, performing them again and again...until they became a natural, unconscious habit. As Cruise said, "You train and drill every aspect over and over and over."[119] You arrive at the point where you no longer have to think about performing—you just perform.

Because he had *lived* this jump so many times before, when the time came for the cameras to roll, Cruise nailed his perilous jump on the very first take. He sailed over the edge of the cliff, and as the crew waited for his parachute to open, Cruise easily landed on the ground below with a smile on his face. His steadfast training had paid off.

Cruise's conscious choices early on and his self-determination to repeat his training again and again is much like our own EntreHabits. If we know what we want and are determined to make it happen, we must first repeat our desired habit at the conscious level. Remember the importance of practice in order to deepen one's EntreGrit. To create unconscious habits, intentional practice is required. By practicing and tapping into our grit, over time, the action becomes a part of our unconscious. It becomes embedded in what we do and who we are. It has become a true habit.

The Unconscious 43 Percent

As Wendy Wood points out in her book *Good Habits, Bad Habits: The Science of Making Positive Habits Stick,* 43 percent of our everyday actions are conducted unconsciously. This means we perform 43 percent of what we do daily without any conscious thought.[120] For example, do you have to think about brushing your teeth in the morning, or do you just do it?

As we seek to create EntreHabits (those daily actions that will fuel our performance), we need to recognize that to become a habit, an action needs to be automatic and unconscious. If it's not, then it's not a habit. James Clear, author of *Atomic Habits: An Easy and Proven Way to Build Good Habits and Break Bad Ones,* describes habits as routines or practices performed regularly.[121] They are automatic responses to specific situations, such as closing your garage door after you pull in your car. We don't think about these actions—we simply do them. Habits should not require our focused attention or conscious thought. Only when an action becomes unconscious is it truly a habit.

Humans tend to deemphasize the importance of our unconscious habits in favor of our deliberate actions. Psychology even has a term for this: "introspection illusion." Our introspection illusion refers to people's cognitive bias that overestimates the influence our conscious intentions and desires have on our responses and behaviors.[122] While our introspection illusion would have us believe our conscious actions invariably shape the outcome of our lives, as Wood's research points out, 43 percent of the time, our unconscious habits drive our outcomes.[123]

Wood demonstrates the danger of focusing solely on our conscious efforts when she writes,

If our noisy, egotistical consciousness takes all the credit for our actions of our silent habitual self (unconscious habits), we'll never learn how to properly exploit this hidden resource (the 43%). Habits will be a silent partner, full of potential energy but never asked to perform to their fullest. Our conscious self's intrusion is keeping us from taking advantage of our habits.[124]

When we fail to understand the importance of our habits, we fail to reach our full potential. As entrepreneurs, we need to tap into the 43 percent and learn to leverage our unconscious habits to grow our character, strengths, and virtues. At their core, our EntreHabits are the positive habits we implement to cultivate what matters most—our character, strengths, and virtues.

EntreHabits CRAWL: Turn Your Character Strengths into the 43 Percent

In 2004, a common language of human strengths was uncovered by psychologists Christopher Petersen and Martin Seligman. They led a group of fifty-five scientists who collaborated to answer the question: What's best about human beings?[125] These scientists traversed the globe to discover the answer and found a common language shared by all of us—twenty-four human strengths ranging from creativity to kindness and bravery to humor. These were found in people around the world.

Positive psychology has one of the longest-standing assessments of these twenty-four character strengths, which can be found at **https://EntreThrive.pro.ViaSurvey.org/**. As the chart below shows, these twenty-four character strengths are linked to six virtues. According to Aristotle, virtues are the "Golden Mean," of how we should be and live. For example, courage lies between reck-lessness and cowardice. Virtues tap into both our moral habits and our intellectual tendencies. However, all virtues are not necessarily gifts at birth but rather must be developed and cultivated by habit. These virtues, with their accompanying strengths, can become the 43 percent, if we bring greater awareness to them in our lives.

VIRTUES	THE 24 CHARACTER STRENGTHS AND THEIR CORRESPONDING VIRTUES				
WISDOM	CREATIVITY	CURIOSITY	JUDGMENT	LOVE OF LEARNING	PERSPECTIVE
COURAGE	BRAVERY	HONESTY	PERSEVERANCE	ZEST	
HUMANITY	KINDNESS	LOVE	SOCIAL INTELLIGENCE		
JUSTICE	FAIRNESS	LEADERSHIP	TEAMWORK	SELF-REGULATION	
TEMPERANCE	FORGIVENESS	HUMILITY	PRUDENCE	HUMOR	SPIRITUALITY
TRANSCENDENCE	APPRECIATION OF BEAUTY	GRATITUDE	HOPE		
WWW.VIACHARACTER.ORG					

By taking the assessment, you'll discover your top five character strengths. To be considered one of your character strengths, the VIA Institute of Character says the trait must possess the following three elements:[126]

1. Essential—The strength feels essential to who you are as a person.

2. Effortless—When you use strengths, it's natural and ef-fortless.

3. Energizing—Using your strength energizes and uplifts you. It leaves you feeling happy, in balance, and ready to take on more.

Turning Our Strengths into Unconscious Choices

One of my wife's key signature strengths is self-regulation, which is part of the temperance virtue. This strength shows up daily for her, whether it be around the house, exercising, or learning something new. Heather is extremely self-disciplined in the way she uses her time, energy, and resources. For example, the kitchen is often clean before the meal is even ready. Once she uses an ingredient, it is put away before she picks up another. The same unconscious habit applies to clothing, books, papers, etc. She automatically puts things away before she moves onto something else. Outside of our kids' rooms or their own messes (that's their responsibility to clean), nothing in our house piles up. Hence, there are rarely big messes she or I need to come back to and clean up later. When making a meal, this saves her time and creates a positive environment for all of us to enjoy. This is not because she feels obligated or pressured by anyone, but rather she has cultivated this area of her signature strength to where it seems to just happen in the background, without any conscious thought or additional mental energy to make it happen.

Ryan Niemiec, the author of *Character Strengths Interventions: A Field Guide for Practitioners*, has noted that to achieve anything in life, whether professionally, personally, or relationally, we must tap into our character strengths.[127] These traits come easily to us, which makes them our strengths. We don't have to work hard to exhibit them, but they naturally flow out of us.

Once we discover our signature character strengths, we can begin to ask ourselves:

- How might I tap into my strengths to create more meaningful relationships?

- How might I use my strengths to solve problems at work?

- What are daily activities I can consciously start doing now that will help strengthen a signature strength of mine and eventually turn it into an unconscious positive habit?

There is also a significant association between character strengths and positive outcomes. Cultivating and focusing on our strengths creates a domino effect on our life. An increase in personal flourishing, health, and life satisfaction will be the end result of such intentional actions.

Because these strengths come naturally and are often driven by unconscious habits, we fail to pay attention to them. However, our signature character strengths often make up part of Wendy Wood's 43 percent of our habitual (unconscious) activities. When we realize these traits and habits will likely shape our future growth, identity, and well-being, we will focus on cultivating them, instead of correcting our weaknesses. The key is to create positive habits that continue to grow our signature character strengths even more.

Harnessing the Power of Our Character Strengths

Paula Toledo is an experienced entrepreneur, founder of SocialWell Collective, musician, writer, speaker, master of Applied Positive Psychology, and key contributor to the research found throughout this book. Below, Paula shares her personal story of how her signature character strengths were just enough light to help her navigate the sudden and tragic death of her husband.

It was 3 a.m. Even if I could sleep, I wouldn't be able to sleep. It was feeding time. My four-week-old newborn was squirming, letting out hungry cries. As I gently cradled him in my arms, I tiptoed to the rocking chair, careful not to wake my two-year-old toddler who was nestled in a bed next to me. As I nursed my son, my mind, like a rock launching into a glass window, spun a million circular thoughts. Emanating and breaking outwards, my thoughts were racing—how could this be? How could he be gone? How could our life be obliterated through one singular event? Losing my husband weeks after our youngest son was born, months away from losing my mother to her battle with cancer, triggered a sense of awe in me. I was in the presence of something vast that I simply could not understand. And yet this feeling of awe was unlike most feelings of awe I had experienced in the past. The feeling was anything but positive. This mysterious, petrifying, and foreboding feeling consumed me.

A sudden soothing sensation on my neck stopped those thoughts and feelings dead in their tracks. I felt a warm light touch, a stroking sensation on my collarbone. As I looked down to see what it was, I saw my son and his tiny newborn fingers moving back and forth in a rhythmic motion. Tears streamed down my face in the presence of an epiphany. I realized that just as life can pull the rug out from under you, in a split moment, it could easily surprise you with love, beauty, and abundance. From that moment forward, I woke up excited to be surprised by life, looking forward to turning the next corner and colliding with wonder and the joyful feast of life.

Awe, wonder, the appreciation for beauty, and hope became way-points for me to decide which corners to turn. They became a constellation of stars, providing just enough light to lead me out of the dark and into thoughtful and meaningful actions. I began playing with my children. Enraptured in their wondrous states, their wonder became contagious, prompting me to write and make music on my own and with others. I started advocating for the use of wonder in our lives, giving a TEDx talk and speaking about the power of play with Roblox at Collision conference. I embarked on further learning and completed my master's in Applied Positive Psychology at the University of Pennsylvania so I could gather evidence-based ways for people and organizations to use art, humanities, and nature to socially connect, foster better relationships, and elevate well-being. It turns out that this constellation is a cluster of my signature character strengths. Unbeknownst to me at the time, leaning into my strengths of love, hope, and appreciation for beauty and excellence helped me to stay resilient so I could rebuild a beautiful life for myself and my family.

Paula's powerful story illustrates how she had regularly operated in her signature character strengths, so she naturally turned to them during her moment of greatest need. In speaking with her further about her story, leaning into her signature strengths was somewhat effortless and natural, sometimes even unconscious.

Here's a quick word of caution: once we identify our signature character strengths, we must be mindful not to overuse or underuse them. When we underuse our strengths, we become complacent. We allow unconscious bad habits, uncertainties, and challenges to take over and weaken our signature character strengths.

On the other hand, we can overuse our strengths. For example, one of my signature character strengths is leadership, and I can go too far with this strength if I assume I need to be the leader each time I'm with a team of people. Sometimes, I may not be the appropriate person to lead. If I took over as the leader every time I had an opportunity, I would lose credibility and trust with my team, family, and others in my life.

Regardless of your signature character strengths, all twenty-four VIA strengths can one day become your strengths as well. You simply need to cultivate them. For instance, if I wanted "persistence" as a signature strength, I could create positive, natural habits that would help grow that trait in me.

EntreHabits WALK: Dynamic Positive Habits

I have come up with the term "Dynamic Positive Habits" to describe my effortless actions that are directly tied to growing one of the twenty-four VIA Character Strengths. This is how I differentiate these types of habits from regular habits. I want to be deliberate when using positive habits to grow my character strengths.

Like all habits, Dynamic Positive Habits are enacted at the subconscious level, which means they work on autopilot. The true power behind the Dynamic Positive Habit is that it allows us to have a built-in system to continue growing in our strengths even when life throws us a curveball. This is why I added the adjective "dynamic," to the term. For example, I have recently decided to create the habit of purposefully texting at least one of my children every day. Remember, I have six children, so this is a stretch goal for me! The current character strength I am working to cultivate the most right now is "love." As a busy entrepreneur, I know that uncertainties are par for course and can get in the way of my most important relationships. Therefore, the Dynamic Positive Habit of texting my kids is something that doesn't take much time but is meaningful to them and deepens the love between us. The challenge is turning this into an unconscious choice, where I automatically text one of my kids throughout the day. However, it is possible.

Three Elements of Dynamic Positive Habits

As psychologist Wendy Wood teaches, three key elements foster our habits: context, repetition, and rewards.[128] On the flip side, the same three elements also hold true for our bad habits. Let's unpack each one.

Context

Not surprisingly, our Dynamic Positive Habits flourish within the right context and environment. The goal is to make our habits easy to do and with the least amount of friction that would impair the unconscious habit.

Making our habits easy to implement goes hand-in-hand with the "effortlessness" of a character strength. Remember, positive habits must be in the context of being effortless if we are to repeat them.

Another reason context matters is that our context (environment) gives us cues about what we should do next. These cues tee up our response, and they can tee up our habits as well.

James Clear notes that we need an "Implementation Intention" to help us leverage our cues.[129] This means we plan beforehand about when and where to perform a certain habit. Researchers Thomas Webb and Paschal Sheeran found that implementation intentions are effective self-regulatory (a character strength) tools because they help us identify the cue faster and with a greater deal of accuracy.[130] For example, the cue for texting my kids might be a phone alarm I set up beforehand, during which I am confident I have thirty seconds to shoot off a text. Having a phone is not enough of a cue to remind me to text. The alarm helps me leverage this cue better. Overtime, the hope is that I won't need this implementation intention anymore and I will unconsciously choose to text one of my kids when I have a small gap in my day.

When we intentionally use cues to tee up our Dynamic Positive Habits, these habits help us grow our signature character strengths. In time, we unconsciously run this chain reaction in the background.

Repetition

The more you repeat your Dynamic Positive Habit, the probability of forming a habit increases substantially. In the texting my kids example, I may have to remind myself and rely on my alarm cue for a while. However, at some point, this repetition will turn into an unconscious habit. As Wendy Wood states,

Until we have laid down a habit in neural networks and memory systems, we must willfully decide to repeat a new action again and

again, even when it's a struggle. At some point, it becomes second nature, and we can sit back and let autopilot drive.[131]

Reward/Purpose

The third and final element of Dynamic Positive Habits is reward. Here, we decide on a reward that makes us happy, and this encourages us to repeat the activity. Over time, as Wood notes, your dependence on the reward will decrease, making your habit independent.[132]

For entrepreneurs, I believe all of our positive habits are best driven by our Guiding Truths, as discussed in EntreClarity. My Dynamic Positive Habit of texting my kids, growing my character strength of love, aligns with several of my Guiding Truths, especially "my family receives my time." As Wood writes, our habits must tie to a deeper purpose or else we'll lose interest.[133] The greatest of all rewards for an entrepreneur happens when our habits align with fulfilling our Guiding Truths. When we see these fulfilled, what reward could be better?

Along with fostering our signature character strengths, Dynamic Positive Habits can also be used to make our breakaways possible. Our breakaways tie to our purpose and move us towards our better, future selves. Each breakaway should also inspire Dynamic Positive Habits. By harnessing the power of Dynamic Positive Habits, we can propel ourselves toward our future self as we seek to grow day by day, week by week, all by implementing habits that lead to profound change.

EntreHabits RUN: The Character Strength of Self-Regulation

Once we've fostered our Dynamic Positive Habits to help us adjust for uncertainties, we begin to RUN when we learn self-regulation. Self-regulation is one of the twenty-four VIA Character Strengths and refers to our ability to control our behaviors, thoughts, and emotions to achieve our most desired goals and outcomes.[134] Those who self-regulate demonstrate discipline and self-control. Others admire them for their ability to control their reactions to insecurities and disappointments.

In other words, self-regulation, of all the twenty-four strengths, is the one that feeds most into habits. Because it's linked to the virtue of temperance, self-regulation helps you manage habits and protect against excess. It is the fertile soil for positive habits, and without it, our habits never fully take root.

While self-regulation aids in the creation of good habits, it also helps to diminish bad ones. Research indicates people with high self-regulation:[135]

- report less anxiety and depression

- better control their anger

- get along better with others

- experience better personal adjustment

- possess greater self-acceptance and self-esteem in relationships

Self-regulation and grit go together like hand and glove. To form a positive habit, we must willingly struggle and passionately persist (implementing our self-regulation and grit), until the action finally becomes a habit.

Growing in Self-Regulation

This past summer, my third child, Jantzen, decided to pursue door-to-door sales to earn money for college. He sold home security systems for a national company and, in the end, became the top selling rookie for the company and one of the top sales reps overall. An impressive accomplishment, especially since we took him away from selling for ten days to join us for a family trip. For anyone his age, selling door to-door in the heat of the humid summer (he sold in Little Rock, AR), requires not only grit but a routine that supports consistent performance. Many young adults who attempt door-to-door sales struggle staying out, as their desire to have a social life kicks in.

If you ask my son, his daily unconscious habits were the differentiating factor between a top sales rep and a mediocre one. Recently, during a company-wide presentation, the owner of the company praised Jantzen and said he knew he could call him at any time during the day and would know where he was. For example, in the mornings, at a certain time, he knew Jantzen would be working out at the gym. Without fail.

I recently asked Jantzen what practices he put in place to help him perform at such an impressive level. I promise I did not coax him for certain answers. This is a summary of his response:

1. Followed a routine and stuck with it. He needed to get out of bed and hit the gym first thing in the morning because doing something "hard" right away paves the path for the rest of the day. (Obviously, the company owner noticed this habit).

2. Delayed gratification was crucial. He would not allow himself to grow complacent with just one sale and then go home. He knew there were more opportunities to sell, so he regulated his celebrations and complacency throughout the day.

3. He quoted Jonathan Byrd, "the man who loves walking will walk further than the man who loves the destination." Then, he said he fell in love with the process of selling and talking with people more than the actual destination of the sale.

In a nutshell, he saw his daily discipline as the cornerstone of his future success.

One disappointment I experienced after taking the VIA Character Strengths Survey was that *self-regulation* wasn't a signature character strength of mine. Meaning, it wasn't in my top five strengths. However, the good news is we can improve our signature character strengths AND those other strengths that might not come quite so naturally by growing in self-regulation.

For entrepreneurs, life's distractions, uncertainties, and even our own emotions can get in the way of our positive habits. Here are six ways to grow the strength of self-regulation. The first five come from Tayyab Rashid, and the sixth derives from my own research and experience:[136]

1. Eliminate Digital Distractions

When doing any deep work, try to work without digital distractions. They simply cause your work to take longer. Here's a great opportunity to practice self-control.

2. Remove Objects of Temptations

This tip simply puts common sense into action. If you want to reign in your spending, then leave your credit cards at home. If you want to abstain from alcohol, don't socialize in bars. While this tip is obvious, it's still violated all of the time.

3. Focus on the Positive

Pay attention to when negative emotions rear their ugly heads and try to focus on the positive attributes of the situation. By learning to self-regulate your anger, you'll avoid displaying your negative responses to others.

4. Utilize Implementation Intentions

As previously mentioned, this can help you generate more self-control by diminishing negative habits and growing positive ones.

5. Discover Your Peak Times

Gain awareness of when you're the most alert for important tasks and projects. Performing tasks when feeling tired, hungry, or disengaged creates an environment where bad habits can take over. Even worse, they can derail our most significant work.

6. Delay Gratification

Self-regulation requires impulse control. To create any kind of positive habit, we must learn to resist immediate gratification or impulsive actions. By delaying gratification, we grow our self-regulation, which subsequently helps grow our other desired character strengths. My son used this principle to keep him knocking on doors, avoiding the gratification one sale might bring, and which him from going back to his apartment early.

EntreHabits FLY: Self-Determined Habits

EntreHabits are the culmination of our signature character strengths. We improve our strengths and grow closer to the Good

Life when we engage in Dynamic Positive Habits. In essence, our habits build our strengths. Our strengths build the Good Life.

Undergirding it all—the Good Life, our strengths, and our habits—is self-regulation. And to grow in self-regulation, we must find the self-determination to follow through with those activities that strengthen it.

As mentioned in EntreClarity, researchers and renowned psychologists Richard Ryan and Edward Deci developed the Self-Determination Theory (SDT) to describe the ideal environment for motivation. They found three core elements drive intrinsic motivation.[137]

Here's how these core elements of SDT can apply to entrepreneurs:

- **Autonomy** can provide entrepreneurs the motivation to pursue their character strengths based on their own goals and purpose—not anyone else's.

- **Competence (or Mastery)** can provide the motivation to stick with a desired positive activity that we want to become a habit. Mastery denotes a level of expertise, a Unique Ability®, a powerful concept taught by Strategic Coach®, that feels effortless and doesn't require much conscious thought.

- **Relatedness** can help us establish meaningful relationships that support our desire to grow our EntreHabits and become better. These can be accountability partners, deep relationships, or even high-quality connections.

When we have self-determination (or motivation), we grow in self-regulation. Our self-regulation then enables us to develop the Dynamic Positive Habits that foster our character strengths. By walking in our character strengths, we are on the right path to creating our own Good Life.

Next Actions

Here's a challenge as you begin to build your EntreHabits: take the VIA Character Strength Survey at our unique page: **https: //EntreThrive.pro.ViaSurvey.org/** . (This will take about 5–10 minutes.) After taking the survey, do the following four steps:

1. Evaluate your five signature character strengths and identify one you want to strengthen.

2. Write down routine positive habits, coupled with Dynamic Positive Habits, which will help cultivate this strength. Keep your habits to less than five.

3. Write down two or more Implementation Intentions/Cues that will help you repeat these positive habits daily.

4. Write how each of these positive habits ties to your pur-
pose/reward. What benefits come from turning these
positive activities into habits?

Now that we understand how our EntreHabits help us grow in
our signature character strengths and fulfill our Guiding Truths,
let's examine the Law of EntreVigor—how the energy we create
helps us create the Good Life.

**The Science Behind the Law of EntreHabits and How
It Can Help You to Create Your Good Life**

**Habits mediate behaviors that help entrepreneurs
live congruently to who they are and how they would
like to live.** Cultivating habits that align with our character
strengths can help entrepreneurs to master a virtue, which is
the key to living the Good Life.[21]

**Habits that elevate an entrepreneur's self-determina-
tion can positively impact their well-being.** Studies show
that self-determination can positively impact an individual's
work satisfaction, self-esteem, relationships, physical health,
intrinsic motivation, and ability to achieve their goals.[22]

> **Automating healthy habits helps to automate healthy choices and behaviors,** therebyconserving mental energy, reducing decision fatigue, and allowing entrepreneurs to focus on essential aspects of their life that contribute to their happiness and well-being.[23]

CHAPTER SEVEN

The Law of Entrepreneurial Vigor: EntreVigor

THE ENERGY YOU CARRY CARRIES YOU.

Iron rusts from disuse; water loses its purity from stagnation…even so does inaction sap the vigor of the mind.
—Leonardo da Vinci

"Aaron, what's going on with you? Did you sleep in? Did you stay up late? Did you just not prepare? You had no energy, and I felt you were someplace else mentally."

I had just keynoted at an industry-wide virtual presentation with over five hundred attendees, and this line of questioning came from a close friend who happened to be in attendance. After seeing my presentation, my friend called me out of concern, and his words about the presentation rang true. I did lack energy. I was somewhere else mentally. Something *was* going on with me.

Trust me, my presentation didn't fail because I lacked virtual speaking skills. I had given many highly rated virtual presentations up to that point. It failed because I lacked vigor and passion—I had become burned out. In 2015, my business was plateauing, fear and worry were chipping away at my stamina, replacing it with brain fog and sleep deprivation. Any little energy I did have was spent speaking at conferences all over the country. Unfortunately, while I'd been pouring myself into my business, I wasn't taking care of myself. My physical health took a hit. My mental health was at an all-time low. The faith I had in my business was slowly slipping through my fingers. I wanted to give up. The constant travel, financial stress, uncertainties, and weakening personal relationships were taking their toll. With the odds seemingly against me, how could I possibly find the vigor and energy to make any positive changes? I was sinking, afraid there would be no lifeboat to pull me out of these crashing waves.

Referring to my Alaska metaphor in the introduction, I was stuck in a perpetual repeat of days 3 & 4.

My friend's feedback was a much-needed wake-up call. Others were noticing on the outside what I was feeling on the inside. I was still tired but I needed to find the strength within myself to get out of this pit. So, I reflected on my current state. How was my health? My mind? My energy? In essence, how was my vigor? Instead of thriving, I was in a cycle of "existing." I needed to find a way to break the cycle or I feared the consequences could be catastrophic for not only me but for my family as well.

Breaking this "existing" cycle must always begin in the mind. Once our minds are free, we, too, can become free. We can get back to where we started—where our dreams were big and our energy, passion, and vigor matched the enormity of those dreams. We can have EntreVigor.

EntreVigor CRAWL: Taming the Mustang Mind

The English word *mustang* derives from the Spanish *mestengo*, and it means that which is wild, stray, or has no master.[141] I thought this was fitting, and it seems to parallel the entrepreneur's mind when it loses focus and strays from working on the Good Life, creating opportunity, and living in abundance. Operating without a master and living a wild existence might sound fun for a while, but our minds can, in turn, grow wild and out of control, leading to a life of chaos. Similar to how I was feeling in 2015.

For the entrepreneur, the *Mustang Mind* represents our busy, distracted, sometimes obsessive, overly stimulated, and even addictive minds.

The *Tamer* of our wild Mustang Minds is our present self. The tamer consciously works to ensure his mental state doesn't veer out of control. The tamer also uses his unconscious positive habits to help control wild Mustang Minds.

Through the ages, people have always been keen to the importance of guarding their minds. When we recognize consequences that come from allowing our minds to wander wherever they desire, we refrain from indulging them. As American entrepreneur Jim Rohn said, "Stand guard at the door of your mind."[142] In his book, *As a Man Thinketh*, James Allen explores the connection between what we think and the direction our lives ultimately take. Allen writes

As he thinks, so he is; as he continues to think, so he remains...for you will always gravitate toward that which you, secretly, most lov e.[143]

As Allen points out, what we secretly love has the ability to protect our minds and keep them positively engaged. On the flip side, it also can slowly destroy our minds, depending on what it is that we love.

Trademarks of a Mustang Mind

Traditionally, entrepreneurs possess a Mustang Mind, and this mindset includes a variety of negative actions and attitudes such as:

- self-doubt

- seeking approval from others

- blaming others

- comparing ourselves to other entrepreneurs

- experiencing negative emotions such as anger (this is different from sitting in our sadness or grief, which can help us heal)

- ruminating thoughts where we go over something again and again (and again)

- chasing shiny objects, distractions, or other mindless pursuits that numb the mind

- addictive behavior that can destroy our relationships, well-being, and overall happiness. This issue alone can turn a Mustang Mind into a wild bucking Bronco

- pursuing anything that draws the mind away from our well-being and goals

The Mustang Mind also tends to state negative thoughts as facts and then adds on an extra reason or "because" to support the negative thought. Here are a few negative "facts" you'll hear escape the mouth of someone with a Mustang Mind:

- I don't deserve their praises because...

- I don't belong here because...

- I don't think they liked me much because...

- They wouldn't want to partner with me because...

- I can't lift squat because...

- I didn't finish that race because...

- I will never learn this topic because...

- I don't need their help anyway because...

- I am not cut out for being an entrepreneur because...

In short, the Mustang Mind allows itself to run wild. While it's great to dream, we must also do the work required to fulfill our dreams. Otherwise our wild, Mustang Minds will merely gaze off into the horizon without ever taking steps to a desired destination.

Learning to Tame the Mustang Mind

The documentary film *Wild Horse, Wild Ride* highlights the Extreme Mustang Makeover Challenge, where one hundred horse trainers—both professional and amateur—attempt to train a wild mustang in only one hundred days. The difficult task mirrors the entrepreneur who seeks to tame his own Mustang Mind. It's truly a wild, unpredictable ride. As one of the horse trainers in the film says, "We work every day, and some days are great and some days are horrible."[144]

As we work on taming our own Mustang Minds, it will require our daily effort and attention. Just like the task of training a wild mustang, we must recognize we attempt no easy feat. We, too, will have good days followed by bad ones. However, there are many things we can do, from eating a better diet to getting enough sleep, which can help tame our minds.

The following chart illustrates the parallels between how one tames a wild mustang and how we begin taming the Mustang Mind.[145]

The Wild Mustang	The Mustang Mind
Provide for your horse's needs.	Care for your physical health (consider your sleep, diet, and exercise patterns).
Let your wild horse come to you.	Practice emotional regulation and let your Mustang Mind come to the present on its own.
Introduce grooming and haltering.	Introduce reading ten pages a day, five-minute meditations, and other small EntreHabits that deepen your character strengths.
Transfer your bonding skills.	Once your Mustang Mind bonds with your conscious, present mind and mirrors its desired habits, you can practice turning those habits into unconscious choices. See EntreHabits for more on this.
Continue introducing new elements and training.	Your Mustang Mind is now ready for new habits and will pick them up faster than ever before. For example, add meditation to your daily positive habits to help further your training.
Be patient and empathetic.	Give your Mustang Mind grace when it strays or becomes wild, all the while showing it that your present mind is the master.

As you can see from the chart, taming the Mustang Mind (or a wild mustang) is a process that begins with small habits and slowly works its way up to larger ones. Habits and vigor are inseparable.

At its core, the Mustang Mind is truly the mind of an entrepreneur. The Mustang Mind must know that its self-aware, present self—the Tamed Mind—is in charge. Just as the wild mustang must submit to its caring trainer who has its best interest at heart, taming our Mustang Minds also requires grace, as we forgive ourselves when we stray off course. Remember, the Mustang Mind desires to repeat negative thoughts, behaviors, and self-doubt if it feels it can do so without being "checked" by the tamed mind. The Tamed Mind (our present self-aware mind) protects the Mustang Mind from running wild and causing damage to itself.

As entrepreneurs, we will always have Mustang Mind instincts that will require a present, conscious mind to keep it tame. It's in that conscious attentiveness we find growth and, ultimately, greater EntreVigor, because positive energy starts in the mind.

EntreVigor WALK: Emotional Regulation of the Mustang Mind

When we think back to our early memories as a child, often we can only remember those emotionally charged moments, when something incredibly wonderful (or terrible) occurred. This kind of memory-making isn't surprising, as molecular biologist Dr. John Medina points out in *Brain Rules: 12 Principles for Surviving and Thriving at Work, Home, and School*:

Emotionally charged events are better remembered for longer, and with more accuracy, than neutral events.[146]

According to Medina, the worst kind of stress comes from the negative emotions that fuel feelings of uncertainty, a lack of control, and total helplessness.[147] For those with the Mustang Mind, when we experience these emotionally charged situations, it is easy for our wild, Mustang Mind to take over and go astray, leaving our Tamed Mind in the dust.

For the entrepreneur, emotional regulation is key, as it will help us maintain a Tamed Mind in the midst of life's chaos. Drs. Martin Seligman and Gabriella Kellerman define emotional regulation in their book *Tomorrowmind* as, "the ability to manage our emotions, positive or negative, in healthy ways that lead us to achieving our dreams and goals."[148] Without emotional regulation, our Mustang Mind is on the loose, but with it, we can handle life's uncertainties and accomplish our dreams in the process.

The ENERGE Mindset Practice: A Positive Intervention for Emotional Regulation

Our Mustang Minds are irrational, at best, and if we allow them to take over, these irrational minds can form negative beliefs about ourselves, our relationships, and the world in general. Mustang Minds also tend to reframe our past into negative memories and experiences, holding us back from happiness now and in the future. Learning to regulate and tame the Mustang Mind is imperative to our well-being as entrepreneurs.

Decades ago, one of the most well-known psychotherapists, Albert Ellis, developed what is known as rational emotive behavior therapy, or REBT. The purpose of REBT is to help one reframe their beliefs about situations, events, and circumstances. REBT has taken on various forms over the years but its principles and practices are still effective today. The therapy incorporated what Ellis refers to as the ABCDE Model of REBT, which created a structured approach to understanding and then changing irrational beliefs. ABCDE stands for (A) Activating Event, (B) Belief or interpretation about the event, (C) Consequence or reaction to the event, (D) Dispute or questioning of the event, and (E) Effect, where you change the irrational belief and replace it with a new healthier one.[149]

What follows is my own ENERGE (not misspelled) Mindset Practice that's inspired by REBT, designed to tame the entrepreneurs' Mustang Mind and create positive energy towards situations, circumstances, and events. It's my own way of remembering how to reframe my past and create a more positive future. Much of it is in line with REBT, with a couple additions I have found very useful.

Events — These are the facts surrounding our past and present events.

Narrative — Our immediate interpretation of the facts from our past and present events. The narrative is our interpretation of the event and the story we immediately tell ourselves, which is often not the one we necessarily want. We tend to attach our present thoughts to a past event, rewriting the story, for better or for worse.

Emotions — These are the emotions (positive or negative) that result from our narrative. This is where the Mustang Mind can take over and run wild with the narrative. At this point, if negative emotions arise (such as anger, fear, resentment, jealousy, etc.), the next three steps help us change the narrative and experience positive emotions.

Recognition — Here we take a step back and pay attention to our current line of thinking and how it affects our past/present events. Once we recognize our thoughts and the subsequent emotions they fuel, we can then choose to respond differently. We can reframe our thoughts about past events, even some of the most challenging ones. Referring back to my Alaska trip, if I framed days 3 & 4 as negative experiences, it would potentially block me from anything that could be learned and gained from the experience. Keeping me from even enjoying days 5 & 6.

Gain — This is the new, positive narrative we gain when we recognize the thoughts fueling our emotional state. This outcome results from training our Mustang Mind to produce thoughts that drive positive emotions such as gratitude, love, compassion, etc. rather than framing past and even present events as negative, which fosters a fixed mindset. This concept was inspired and created by Dan Sullivan of Strategic Coach®, the author of the best-selling book, *The Gap and The Gain*.

Energy – The tamer of a wild mustang knows that hidden beneath the horse's wild exterior are untapped positive characteristics that create fresh positive energy. Positive energy is the desired outcome of taming my Mustang Mind.

EntreVigor RUN: Mind and Body Alignment

The next step to growing in our EntreVigor is understanding the importance of mind and body alignment. As we grow older, we assume our bodies will slowly decay over time, but, as authors Chris Crowley and Dr. Henry Lodge write in *Younger Next Year*, it doesn't have to be that way. As Crowley and Lodge put it, "Decay is optional."[150] According to the authors, our bodies and minds are designed to work in tandem with each other, and when the two align, it helps us build a better life with those we most love.

To achieve anything of significance in life, our minds and bodies must be in sync with one another. One cannot thrive without the other, so we need to concern ourselves with making sure both our bodies and our minds are flourishing. For example, cycling is one of the tools I personally use to sync both my mind and my body. For me, it's not about merely getting physical exercise—it's a form of meditation. According to MensLine Australia, a free counseling service, cycling is an especially excellent activity for positive mental health. For example, cycling improves your mood and memory, calms you down, helps you sleep better, and improves your creative thinking, among other benefits.[151] In fact, exercising and being in nature have such a profound effect on the mind that they're considered a key therapeutic to combat anxiety, stress, and depression.

We see countless books on the topics of exercise, diet, and improving one's overall health, and while I don't pretend to be an expert on the topics, I can certainly provide the evidence as to why taking care of our bodies and minds is so important to an entrepreneur's overall well-being. I will, however, let you do your own exploration on these topics. The research is quite convincing; to go the distance, we need to take care of our bodies *and* our minds.

I think it is false to believe that vigor starts with our bodies. As stated earlier, EntreVigor begins and ends with the mind. When we adopt the Good Life mindset, our bodies will fall in line with that mindset.

Your Mind Must Be the Master Trainer

When we allow our Mustang Mind to run wild, our bodies become the trainers of our minds. For me, this is when I eat too many potato chips or gorge myself at an all-you-can-eat buffet. That's not good, and for many, allowing the body to control the mind can be disastrous to their well-being. When that happens, we don't operate on rational choices, but on impulse. This is where overeating, addiction, and poor health start. The importance of taming our Mustang Mind first is essential, because until we do, our body rules our mind, as opposed to our minds ruling our bodies.

In the book *Breaking the Habit of Being Yourself*, Dr. Joe Dispenza unpacks the synchronicity of the body and mind when he writes:

There's a certain synchronicity that takes place moment by moment between the brain and the body. In fact, as we begin to feel the way we are thinking—because the brain is in constant communication with the body—we begin to think the way we are feeling. The brain constantly monitors the way the body is feeling...[the brain] will generate more thoughts that produce chemicals corresponding to the way the body is feeling, so that we first begin to feel the way we think and then to think the way we feel.[152]

In short, our mind is rarely in the driver's seat if we have a Mustang Mind. Instead, our body "runs the show," and according to Dispenza, when we allow our feelings from our body to drive the way we think, we are trapped into never thinking bigger than what we currently feel. Read that again. It's deep. *Our body dictates how we think, and we never rise above the way we feel.* Our body becomes the master, throwing our minds into a wild, negative mindset—the Mustang Mind.

For example, as your body naturally ages, if you think you're growing old and allow yourself to ruminate on this, your brain will release chemicals into the body. Before long, you will feel exactly the way you were thinking—old and incapable of pushing yourself to greater health. This happens when our bodies drive our minds because our minds naturally match what is happening in the body. Dispenza notes this can become a dangerous communication loop between mind and body.[153] Here is where many of our negative unconscious habits play out: the body controlling the mind and giving in to unhealthy habits that keep us from creating the Good Life.

Having It All While Not Having It All

Have you ever known someone who simultaneously has it all and *doesn't* have it all? My friend Jerry falls into this category. Jerry is a trailblazer professionally, with a booming business that keeps expanding. He has the right business with the right product at the right time, and his business peers greatly respect him for paving the way. His net worth easily reaches the $50 million plus mark today. In the eyes of most, Jerry has it all.

Unfortunately, it's unlikely Jerry will become all he could be because of his health and other poor choices. Over the years, I've watched Jerry's vigor decline, causing a variety of problems that contribute to his poor health. They are as follows:

- Poor Health

    At just 50 years old, Jerry's health suffers. He is overweight and in poor physical shape. His body rules his mind, resulting in the decline of both.

- His Mustang Mind Runs Wild

His inability to focus his energy in positive ways over the last few years has been difficult for his staff. His lack of direction and clarity in leading his team contributes to a toxic environment. Jerry's Mustang Mind has created this chaos at work. His turnover rates are at an all-time high.

- He Suffers from Burnout

Jerry is displaying all of the signs of entrepreneurial burnout, despite his wealth and business success. He's admitted to me that his burnout is likely causing him to overeat, another unconscious negative habit. This burnout isn't caused by putting in too many hours, quite the contrary. He avoids the office whenever possible because his Mustang Mind, controlled by his body, is calling the shots now and has slowly eroded the passion for work he once loved and felt called to do.

From the outside looking in, it would appear that Jerry "has it all." His wealth puts him easily in the top .05 percent of the wealthiest people in the world, which is phenomenal and should be celebrated. However, Jerry likely won't be around to fully enjoy it. While his bank accounts are full, his mind and body are in decay.

Unless Jerry wakes up and creates EntreVigor to help him sync up his mind and body, he may not make it to his sixtieth birthday. While he has the opportunity to reverse his trajectory, if he does not, Jerry will live short of what is possible for him. He will not enjoy his wealth or his loved ones as much as he could.

Sometimes, despite all of our best efforts, poor health still comes our way, such as with cancer, and it shortens our life's journey. This was the case with my mentor and friend Dale. He was all in on his mind and body alignment, but cancer still found him. In Dale's case, I had to turn to my faith for answers and peace.

However, in Jerry's case, his poor health results from giving in to his body and letting it fuel his Mustang Mind. This is when decay rolls down hill and requires massive action to stop it.

The Synced-Up Entrepreneur

Once we understand the importance of mind and body alignment, we can then begin to sync up our own. Synchronization is defined as, "to cause to go on, move, operate, and work at the same rate and exactly together."[154] Thriving as an entrepreneur requires both the mind and body to move together in an upward, positive trajectory. The synced-up entrepreneur isn't having his mind and body only work together—the pair are pushing each other to grow, thrive, and flourish!

As entrepreneurs, the kind of thriving we seek is eudaimonic, as opposed to the hedonic well-being. While hedonic well-being seeks a life of maximized pleasure, prioritizes enjoyable experiences, and pursues short-term gratification, we aim for something greater—the eudaimonic well-being of a life of self-fulfillment, virtue-oriented living, and the pursuit of long-term flourishing. According to Aristotle, we experience eudaimonia (or flourishing) when we *rationally* pursue what is worthwhile and virtuous in life.[155] As such, when we sync our minds and bodies and the two work together, we can more easily pursue the good and the virtuous. This leads to greater eudaimonia, which for Aristotle, was the Good Life.

Syncing Up Requires Intention

Jen Stengl is the founder of the home care business Golden Harmony. Jen first became interested in creating her own business after discovering she could only go so far working for others. Jen loved the idea of being her own boss because those employee limitations would be removed. As someone who had a soft heart for seniors, Jen wanted to create something to impact the seniors in her community in a beneficial way, along with providing her with work she could truly connect with. Thus, Golden Harmony was started.

Over time, Jen's business evolved and eventually took off. She found her endeavor extremely fulfilling and realized it had excellent growth potential. But then it happened—the business Jen created to give her freedom and a limitless life suddenly felt claustrophobic. Only three years in, Jen felt stuck, overwhelmed, and burned out. Her quality of life began to suffer, as she no longer had much time for her family let alone taking care of herself. Family members reached out to her, sharing their concerns that the demands of Jen's business were affecting her personal life. It was as though she had created a monster, and the monster was consuming her. Jen decided she was going to find a resource who could help her find a solution to the areas that took much of her time. She knew she had to invest in the right people to help her get back in control of her business. To begin to find a better path for the future of the business she courageously reached out to me and before we knew it, we were business partners. When she came to me, she was already taming her Mustang Mind and I just helped her continue that.

Before long, the company was reorganized with the right people who then jumped in and helped create the space she needed for mind and body to sync. Her time is now her own again and the business continues to thrive with exponential growth. While Jen had once believed "The Lie of the Either/Or," she learned she could have both—a great business and a flourishing life. She now feels healthier, eats better, sleeps better, and has time for family, friends, and travel. An important point is that Jen's ability to sync up her body and mind was blocked by the overwhelming responsibilities in her business. Without having the intention, courage, and wisdom to create the space to sync, she may have never turned the corner. For her, the right people helped create that space but sometimes it's more than just the right people. Often, we need to intentionally invest in better processes, systems, and operating business models that create space for entrepreneurs in their businesses, so they can find the time to sync up their mind and body.

I personally recommend the Entrepreneurial Operating System (EOS®) as a great business model for entrepreneurs, as I use it for all my businesses. However, there are others you may want to consider. Go to **EntreThrive.com/Resources**, where we provide resources and recommendations, including EOS and Strategic Coach®.

Syncing Your Mind and Body With Nature

Nature has always captured the heart and imagination of humanity. The nineteenth century English poet Lord Byron wrote about the splendor experienced in the outdoors when he penned,

> *There is a pleasure in the pathless woods,*
> *There is a rapture on the lonely short,*
> *There is society, where none intrudes,*
> *By the deep sea, and music in its roar:*
> *I love not man the less, but Nature more.*[156]

For the busy entrepreneur, it may seem that spending time outdoors is a waste when that time could be spent on more important matters. However, according to a 2019 study, individuals who connect more to nature have a greater eudaimonic well-being and report higher levels of personal growth than those who lack that consistent connection.[157]

We need to consider the importance nature can have on our flourishing. Rest, as it would seem, is not a waste. As John Lubbock famously wrote,

Rest is not idleness, and to lie sometimes on the grass under trees on a summer's day, listening to the murmur of the water, or watching the clouds float across the sky, is by no means a waste of time.[158]

Some of my greatest business ideas have come while I spent time in nature, and below are some of my best practices to sync up both body and mind with nature:

- A Birthday Tradition

  Every September, on my birthday, I spend an entire day by myself in a remote river area, thinking, walking, wading for miles, fishing, and again thinking (in that order). It's my birthday gift to myself—a time to sync my mind and body. Catching and releasing fish is a side benefit.

- Intentional Nature Walks...and Rides

  Regardless of the temperature, I love to walk along the river and experience great peace and solace. To be honest, sometimes I prefer driving my ATV along this same path. I find peace either way.

- Cycling

  By now, you probably know I like to bike! However, there's nothing like cycling outdoors in the summer. Every year, I ride up to Bogus Basin, a ski resort outside of Boise, Idaho. Climbing 3,500 feet in fifteen miles challenges my body, but it also allows me to be with my thoughts. My mind and body sync up in a real and natural way.

- Problem Solving

> Often, when I do a physical activity, I try to think of a problem I'm working on and allow the synchronization of my mind and body to help solve it. Many times I have come up with solutions to problems I may have otherwise overlooked if I were merely sitting at my desk. Nature awakens my mind, giving it the opportunity to align with my body.

Research has shown that getting in nature requires less of our brain to process creative ideas, because nature is our natural playground, as opposed to being inside four walls where creativity sometimes gets stifled. Would it surprise you that we have terms for this in psychology? They are called *attention-restoration theory* and *perceptual-fluency account*.[159] Basically, these theories support the idea that nature can awaken our attention more effortlessly, simplify the way we process information, and decrease our stress.

The lesson here is to get out in nature—rain or shine—and do so with an activity you enjoy!

EntreVigor FLY: Committing to Our Alignment

Lastly, we FLY in our EntreVigor when we commit to our alignment, when we take it seriously, and when we thoroughly invest it in. For example, in 2016, I committed to aligning my mind and body, beginning with cycling. Not surprisingly, the growth of my company in the same year was exponential. That year, my company began its rocket journey as my newfound vigor carried over into the workplace in a major way. My team felt my energy and responded to it in a positive manner. As a result, only a year after I received that call from my friend after the less-than-engaging presentation, our business grew to levels we hadn't yet seen.

As we learned earlier in EntreHabits, it took Tom Cruise thirteen thousand skydive jumps to prepare both his body and mind for his perilous stunt. We need to recognize that if we, too, want to sync up our minds and bodies, we must engage in daily, positive habits that align the two. Repetition is necessary, for then our mind and body alignment become natural. We won't have to work so hard to be synced up. We'll have in place the habits that run on autopilot that make the aligned life of vigor possible.

EntreVigor Challenge

As you begin to work on your EntreVigor, here is a two-part challenge to help you grow.

Part 1: The ENERGE Mindset Practice

Think of a recent event that was hard to handle and fueled a negative mindset. Run this event through the ENERGE Mindset Practice (see p. 177) and take note of how you feel about the event *before* the practice and how you feel *immediately after*. Did your mindset change, even slightly, toward the positive?

Part 2: Getting Into Nature

This week, schedule at least one physical outdoor activity you enjoy that incorporates both the mind and body. Think of a problem (personal or professional) that you would like to solve during this activity. For example, think of an opportunity you're excited about but still need to figure out how to best capture it. Then, enter into your outdoor activity with the problem in mind and allow the ideas to flow. Bring along a Breakaway Narrative sheet just in case.

Guide Tip: avoid a problem that has a great deal of anxiety surrounding it or the activity won't be as enjoyable.

Next, we come to the final law—the Law of EntreAgency—where we'll unpack the keystone law of EntreThrive.

The Science Behind the Law of EntreVigor and How It Can Help You to Create Your Good Life

Practices in EntreVigor promote metacognition, whichis a higher-order skill whereby a person learns to observe and think about what they are thinking and how it is impacting their emotions and behavior.[20] Metacognition is an important skill, and it can help entrepreneurs to self-reflect, engage in critical thinking about their thoughts and beliefs, and find proactive ways to use their strengths to influence positive outcomes in their lives.

Mental agility and being flexible in thought processes can boost entrepreneurial adaptability, learning, and creativity, and therefore, can support one's well-being. Cognitive behaviors that support greater optimism and growth mindsets can foster resilience. Research indicates that optimism is associated with increased motivation, superior achievement, and better physical health.[21]

Self-regulation, the skills and abilities to manage one's emotions, needs, and desire, is positively correlated with psychological well-being. By regulating their feelings, thoughts, and actions, entrepreneurs not only protect themselves from life disturbances and challenges, but help themselves focus on achieving their desired goals.[22]

CHAPTER EIGHT

The Law of Entrepreneurial Agency: EntreAgency

THE GOOD LIFE YOU DESIRE IS YOUR RESPONSIBILITY TO CREATE.

When do we try hard? When do we break out of our sloth and overcome barriers that seem insurmountable? When do we reach for goals that seem unattainable? When do we persist against the odds? When do we make new, creative departures? These all require Agency, an individual's belief that he or she can influence the world.

—Dr. Martin Seligman

E ntrepreneurs are filled with creativity and imagination, dreaming up futures laced with possibilities. This is part of the reason we became entrepreneurs in the first place—we dream of the freedom it can offer us. Sometimes our hopeful aspirations guide us to exciting innovations and advancements. Other times, we might find ourselves face-planting onto a sidewalk of chosen regrets. The difference between exciting innovations and the sidewalk of chosen regrets is often tied to choices, but not the kind of choices you might think. The choices I am talking about are more about mindset and how you choose to frame past, present, and future experiences. This topic has been interwoven throughout this book because of its critical importance to incorporating the eight laws of EntreThrive, especially when it comes to EntreAgency. If we truly want to create the Good Life, we must understand that part of this creation requires our ability to confidently reframe our past so that it supports a bigger and brighter future. Did you realize you had that kind of power? You do. Let me illustrate.

One of my greatest tests of my personal agency came when I successfully exited a company I had founded and grew for twelve years. I was extremely proud of what we had accomplished as a team and had thoroughly enjoyed the last few years of our journey. I made the choice to sell my majority ownership in order to pursue other interests at the time, specifically an opportunity to partner with a friend of mine, who owned a franchise that was expanding. I approached one of my three other partners, who I knew would be interested in increasing his ownership. I gave him my price and he accepted. I was grateful and we closed the deal in February of 2020, a month before COVID-19 changed our lives forever.

As is the case with some interests, they sometimes don't pan out. The primary reason for selling was to pursue the partnership in the growing franchise business. A few months into negotiations, it became clear that I could not seem to get my interest to grow into a passion, even after considerable practice. Therefore, my EntreGrit fizzled. I decided to part ways the same month my deal finalized in February. I was still running a successful EOS Implementer® coaching business and investing in other opportunities that appealed to me. Life was good, even when that partnership didn't work out.

Though my former company took a dip early in the pandemic, by year's end, it was soaring again. When 2021 came, many private equity firms were ready to invest capital into companies that had weathered the storm, shooting valuations through the roof. My company had been primed for this environment, due to its unique offerings and niche in a growing marketplace. In July of 2021, a private equity firm purchased my former company for a significantly higher valuation than I had settled on just eighteen months earlier.

At first, this was devastating for both me and my wife, knowing we had walked away from millions. My Mustang Mind took over and turned to irrational, pessimistic thoughts. I had framed my past choice to sell, as a negative and completely irresponsible decision on my part.

At this same time, I had been accepted into the Master of Applied Positive Psychology program at the University of Pennsylvania, with the goal of helping entrepreneurs find personal flourishing. I was excited about the opportunity to dig deep into the science and create an entirely new company, designed to make this impact. However, when the news came of the sale of my former company to the equity firm, I allowed it to rob me of the excitement and joy I felt for the program. Thoughts like, "I could have had more money to invest in my new company if I had just held out longer," or even worse, "that was my once-in-a-lifetime opportunity…," and so forth. I was about to dive deep into well-being, while choosing to limit my agency for the future. Taking the words from one of my favorite podcasters, authors, and entrepreneurs, Ed Mylett, I was taking the perspective that life was happening *to* me and not *for* me.

On October 3, 2021, a month into my MAPP studies, my professor, Dr. Martin Seligman, was lecturing on human agency that helped me reframe that experience and many since. For the past few years, Seligman has turned much of his research and focus on the topic of agency and how it affects our overall happiness and well-being. During our class that day, he provided historical context to the ebb and flow of agency throughout the ages, starting from 7000 BC until the time of Saint Augustine, 354-430 AD. That period of time ignited my fascination with the vital role human agency has played throughout our history. When limited, chaos often ensued.

Seligman then spoke of the three elements of agency: (1) self-efficacy, (2) optimism, and (3) imagination. When those three elements are not present, one's free will to choose is limited. Seligman successfully demonstrated that when these three elements were missing in society, so was one's agency, as was the case in the Dark Ages.

When Seligman shared these three elements, it dawned on me that because I was not taking extreme ownership for the way I viewed the sale of my company, I was robbing myself of my self-efficacy, optimism, and imagination. I was choosing to give away my own agency. The more I thought about those three elements, the more I was convinced of their importance in human agency. I began to understand that by choosing to reframe my past, I would grow my belief in myself, my self-efficacy, thus fueling my optimism and imagination. I no longer saw the sale of my company as negative but actually as a steppingstone to my Good Life and new 10X opportunities.

See, if I had continued on as CEO of my company, I wouldn't have had some of the special experiences I have had since, including the MAPP program, partnering with wonderful business partners on new opportunities, started my next 10X company (EntreThrive), identifying these eight laws, and certainly not writing this book that you are reading right now. I have learned that agency isn't just about choices we make about our present and future selves but choices we make about how we see the past. EntreAgency is the keystone law of EntreThrive because without tapping into its strength, all the laws fall short of bringing us to the Good Life.

EntreAgency Defined

EntreAgency is the belief that individuals have the ability to make choices and decisions independently of deterministic forces. Fate and destiny do not rule our lives, but rather, free will captains the ship. Free will suggests people have the capacity to act autonomously without being entirely bound by external influences or predetermined factors.

EntreAgency encompasses the following formula: a combination of Seligman's (father of positive psychology) three components of agency, psychology's concept of prospection, and taking ownership of outcomes.

EntreAgency CRAWL: Channeling Agency into Three Elements

According to Seligman, we unleash our agency when we believe our actions can influence the world. He suggests that the "psychological state of agency causes human progress and the absence of this psychological state causes stagnation."[163] His research highlights how this pattern of causation is repeated throughout the ages within a variety of civilizations. As Seligman notes, agency has three key components that must be present for one to fully maximize their agency (or free will):[164]

1. Self-Efficacy ("I believe I can accomplish a specific goal")

2. Optimism ("I believe I can accomplish this goal far into the future")

3. Imagination ("I believe I can accomplish many goals")

While Seligman refers to agency in general, his insight applies well to the realm of entrepreneurism. His three components can help an entrepreneur channel the power of their agency, giving them positive emotions about their past and the ability to frame their future in the same way.

THE LAW OF ENTREPRENEURIAL AGENCY: ENTREAGENCY199

SELF-EFFICACY'S Role in EntreAgency

Entrepreneurs who have self-efficacy have confidence in themselves as they maintain a belief in their ability to influence their actions and surroundings. They have faith in their capacity to affect a positive outcome in their life. In the absence of self-efficacy, individuals believe external factors dictate their future outcomes, eroding their sense of personal agency. To them, their future, their success, and their life's outcome are, ultimately, out of their hands.

As noted in Seligman's "Agency in Greco-Roman Philosophy," both Plato and Aristotle believed we choose our actions and our desired outcomes.[165] These philosophers believed in human agency and the power of self-efficacy, unlike Saint Augustine who believed humans could not act independently and control their life's outcome. Though some argue Augustine had good intentions, he felt the human race had fallen and was incapable of choosing right. This approach diminished self-efficacy in his followers, limiting their agency.

Like Plato and Aristotle, Seligman's strong belief in human agency leads to progress, while a weak belief leads to stagnation.

As psychologist Albert Bandura writes, "Unless people believe they can produce desired effects by their actions, they have little incentive to act."[166] This belief— self-efficacy—is the foundation of our agency. If you believe you can do it, you'll do everything in your power to do it.

OPTIMISM Is Central to EntreAgency

Up until the late 1980s, psychology mainly focused its efforts and research on ways to alleviate suffering among mental disorders documented and classified in the *Diagnostic and Statistical Manual of Mental Disorders (DSM)*. Within the field was an unbalanced approach whereby researchers looked at what was wrong with humans, such as their negative thinking and maladaptive behaviors. Rarely did researchers explore what types of thinking and behaviors could help humans reach their potential.

In 1998, when Martin Seligman became president of the American Psychological Association, he set out on an initiative to change this focus. What resulted was an area of research called positive psychology. In his previous notable research, Seligman discovered a connection between people who *learn* to be helpless and depression.[167] When people face prolonged stressful circumstances where they believe the outcome is beyond their control, they eventually stop trying to change the outcome, even if they had the means to do so. In other words, they learn to be helpless.

The theory of learned helplessness had a significant impact on the way therapists now treat depression. Seligman proposed that if the behavior of helplessness can be learned, then behaviors like empowering people to gain a sense of control and agency in their lives could also be learned.[168] His research pointed to learning optimistic ways of explaining disturbances and stressful events in our lives. Combined with learning agentic behaviors to change our situation for the better, both positive approaches led to effective interventions to buffer life stressors and also help people to flourish.

As entrepreneurs, we are familiar with the mental fortitude required to stay in the game and see our vision through. With the pressures and high-stakes, limited leisure time with family and friends, and ongoing challenges of running a business, the uncertainty and stress can sometimes take its toll and lean us towards a more pessimistic mindset.

Seligman theorized that if we could learn to think and behave in a manner that exhibited helplessness, we could also learn to think and behave in an optimistic way that helped us to flourish. He classified the way that optimists and pessimists explain events and experiences within a framework called "Three Ps" (Permanence, Pervasiveness, and Personalization).[169]

Explanatory Style	Permanence	Pervasiveness	Personalization
Optimistic	Temporary	Specific	External
Pessimistic	Permanent	Pervasive	Internal

In his groundbreaking book, *Learned Optimism*, Seligman describes optimism and pessimism as explanatory styles.[170] An explanatory style is simply the way we interpret our experiences. How we explain them to ourselves and others. The three Ps are a way to describe the explanatory styles and how optimism differs from pessimism. According to Seligman's research, optimists see challenges as temporary rather than permanent, specific rather than pervasive, and external rather than personal or internal.

Let me share a real-life example to illustrate these two kinds of explanatory styles of optimism and pessimism. I have close friends who have demonstrated an optimistic explanatory style in almost everything I've watched them overcome. Matt and Jane (a married couple) started Pizza Pie Cafe, a successful regional pizza franchise business. Over the years, they have experienced all kinds of personal and professional setbacks that they could have viewed as permanent, pervasive, and internal. Recently, one of their corporately owned location's parking lots was now being shared with newer big box stores. This significantly limited parking for their customers, which eventually caused that location to shut down. When many would have been stuck in the past, they naturally saw this situation as temporary, specific to that location, and externally caused. This optimistic explanatory style has allowed them to fail fast yet move forward time and time again. It is no coincidence that their lives mirror this optimistic approach. They are models of what it means to create your own Good Life.

IMAGINATION Connects EntreClarity to EntreAgency

While self-efficacy and optimism make EntreAgency possible, your agency truly blossoms when imagination is present. Imagination gives an entrepreneur vision for the unseen and unknown. It allows them to dream about a new life, new services, new solutions, and overall, how to make the world a better place. In fact, all the laws leading to this last one require imagination.

As Albert Einstein said, "Imagination is everything. It is the preview of life's coming attractions."[171] However, if we lack clarity on our values, goals, and breakaways, our imagination can run wild (the Mustang Mind) and ultimately cause our EntreAgency to go rogue, moving us forward without boundaries and direction. As Seligman and Kellerman note in their book *Tomorrowmind*, our mindset and innovation (our imagination) have the ability to blind us to the worst-case scenarios of our own ideas.[172]

As creative, imaginative entrepreneurs, we must harness the power of the imagination, while also ensuring it does not lead us astray. One way we do this is through prospection.

EntreAgency WALK: The Prospective Entrepreneur

Prospection, as defined by psychologists, is the mental ability to anticipate and simulate future events, scenarios, or possibilities. It Involves envisioning potential outcomes, making plans, setting goals, and mentally preparing for various situations that have not yet occurred.

The first part of prospection—anticipating and simulating—sums up a day in the life of a thriving entrepreneur. However, many of us have not yet mastered the ability to anticipate, simulate, plan, and imagine future possibilities.

Prospection ties to Seligman's three components of agency because self-efficacy, optimism, and imagination—strengthen an entrepreneur's ability to master prospection. Once entrepreneurs master prospection, their ability to control their future outcomes expands exponentially. They suddenly become the captains of their better, greater, future selves. And their agency—their ability to make choices unrelated to other forces—also expands.

Because EntreAgency is composed of self-efficacy, optimism, and imagination, these three components also fuel our ability to project and evaluate future possibilities, which then gives us the ability to act. One who is limited in these three components of agency would likely be restricted in their ability to:

1. Believe their projections were accurate and actionable **(self-efficacy)**

2. Be **optimistic** about the outcome of their projections, along with their desires/dreams

3. Use their **imaginations** when thinking of these future possibilities

In essence, prospection is a kind of agentic act that expands our freedom to draw upon both the past and present. Referring to the three components of an optimistic explanatory story, how we explain the past and present can be aided by prospection. It allows us to think of exciting, future possibilities that we can act on because we already possess the self-efficacy, optimism, and imagination needed to do so.

The Breakaway Narrative exercise is an excellent positive tool designed to cultivate your imagination and consider the obstacles, possibilities, and catalytic mechanisms that will make your breakaway possible. Refer back to the first law, EntreClarity, and become more familiar with that exercise (see p. 48).

The Courage to Act

Victor Hugo, one of the greatest poets of our time, once famously said, "No army can withstand the strength of an idea whose time has come."[173] When we move forward with our EntreAgency, we must first find the courage to act. While it's important to consider both the best- and worst-case scenarios, we need to be careful to not simply sit in our prospection. Imagination must be our starting point but not our final destination. At the end of the day, we must have the courage to take action on our ideas when we have successfully prospected and are ready to move.

On the flip side, an entrepreneur who struggles with prospecting is a dangerous entrepreneur. They move forward quickly, failing to look before they leap. The well-known conative assessment program, Kolbe A™ Index (kolbe.com), measures how we take action when we are free to be ourselves. I have been using this assessment for many years in all of my businesses. Their primary assessment, the Kolbe A Index, measures four primary areas of action: (1) Fact Finder, (2) Follow Thru, (3) Quick Start, and (4) Implementer. It is measured on a scale of 1–10 and there is no bad score, just scores that work for or against you depending on the function you play in your company.

My Kolbe A Index score is 5 Fact Finder, 3 Follow Thru, 9 Quick Start, and 3 Implementers. I am not going to analyze or break this down here, but just know my score is fairly typical of a visionary entrepreneur. Notice my Quick Start of a 9. I have been comparing my score with hundreds of entrepreneurs who have taken the assessment and, in general, most are between a 7-10 in this category. Going back to the dangers of prospection: vision-ary entrepreneurs are often very high quick-starts. We like to act! This is where we must be careful. By tapping into our prospective capabilities, we can move forward with greater confidence and measured risk.

EntreAgency RUN: Ownership of Outcomes

Once we possess the courage to act, we have to own the out-comes of our choices, whether extraordinary or disappointing. Ownership of outcomes also means we celebrate others' successes. Sometimes as entrepreneurs, we want to take ownership of *all* the outcomes, even those that were the result of a team effort. It's likely other people were involved in our wins, and we should celebrate their contributions.

When my eldest son, Tanner, turned five, my parents came over to celebrate the special occasion. As soon as they walked in the door, my dad gave the birthday boy three dollars. While it was a fun surprise for my son, my thoughts immediately turned to my three-year-old daughter, Brinley, who had witnessed this transaction. Was she going to lose it? I feared she'd want the money and would start saying (or screaming) it wasn't fair.

That's what most three-year-olds would do.

But she didn't. Instead, she ran around the house celebrating. "Dad! Grandma and Grandpa gave Tanner three dollars!" There was no jealousy or comparison. She was genuinely happy for her brother even though she wouldn't benefit from the money. Brinley chose to celebrate someone else's wins and envisioned the great possibilities her brother could buy with those dollars, and her actions taught me something about what thriving truly looks like.

This is what agency is all about—it's taking responsibility for ourselves and the way we think about things. This is what it means to truly thrive. We can only thrive in this life when we're happy for others' successes, but we have to *choose* to be happy for them. While we could spend our lives comparing ourselves to others and noting what they have and what we don't, we can also choose to be happy and even grateful for others' successes.

Pat Summit, one of the greatest women's NCAA basketball coaches, once said, "Responsibility equals accountability equals ownership. And a sense of ownership is the most powerful weapon a team or organization can have."[174] As the entrepreneur and founder of your company, you are responsible for everything that happens in your company—the good, the bad, and the ugly. Agency means we accept that reality and own it *all*.

In the book *Extreme Ownership: How U.S. Navy SEALs Lead and Win*, author Jocko Willink says, "Leaders must own everything in their world. There is no one else to blame."[175] When we take ownership of everything that happens in our lives, we experience limitless freedom.

Owning How You Internalize Opinions from Others

Another important element of taking responsibility for our feelings is not allowing the opinion of others to create a negative opinion of ourselves. My wife and I hang around people who push us physically, mentally, and spiritually. These close friends are our biking buddies, snowshoe partners, hiking companions, and successful entrepreneurs in their own right. Matt and Jane of Pizza Pie Cafe are part of this special group. We have been to the top of mountains together—bicycling, hiking, and snowshoeing. They know me better than most. When they have an opinion of something I've done or said, I listen intently and value their opinions. I feel the same about close family members. I know that when my intimate friends and family share something personal with me, it is almost always out of love and worthy of my ear. Therefore, their opinion of me should be considered.

Considered is the key word. Even then, I don't take their opinion as an absolute truth until I have taken the time to honestly evaluate it. If someone I don't know well expresses their opinion of me via social media, community, or otherwise, I stop listening. As the famous podcaster Tom Bilyeu has said, and I paraphrase, "if you can't text me, your opinion of me doesn't matter." Too often, we choose to let opinions about us, coming from those we don't know well and who don't know us well, influence how we feel about ourselves. If someone really doesn't know you then why should we choose to let their opinions have a seat at the table of our minds?

For nearly two decades, I had built successful businesses in the in-home care space; one of which pushed me into the limelight, where I had the opportunity to make a positive impact on the lives of thousands of entrepreneurial home-care owners. When I exited that company, I continued to be involved, but in the background, investing in other companies in the space, including becoming a partner in an innovative home-care agency in North Carolina.

It was during this same time, I discovered my new calling of helping entrepreneurs flourish personally, along with creating positive cultures, and fully invested my time, money, and energy to learn everything I could about positive psychology, well-being, and thriving for entrepreneurs, including completing a top master's degree in the field of positive psychology. Most of these efforts happened in the background as well, with only those closest to me aware of the great lengths I was going through to go "all in" with my new-found passion and calling.

Fast forward several years to just a few months ago, when I attended a home-care conference and ran into an acquaintance I had helped nearly a decade earlier. She asked what I was doing now and I mentioned I was helping entrepreneurs flourish, build positive cultures, and create the Good Life. Her response: "Interesting. You should just stay with what you know, home care. You'll make so much more money in that space." Bold opinion for someone I hadn't seen in over seven years. Did her opinion matter to me? Not in the least. It was coming from a place of ignorance. Gratefully, I was wise enough to ignore this opinion, but what if I hadn't? What if I had internalized her statement? Choosing to adopt that one opinion could have potentially limited my self-efficacy, optimism, and imagination; it could have even caused me to stop pursuing my passion and calling, including the writing of this book!

Let's do ourselves a favor and choose to ignore opinions about us coming from those who are outside the path of our entrepreneurial journey. It's simply distracting noise that gets in the way of your Good Life.

EntreAgency FLY: EntreAgency Opens the Door to Limitless Possibilities

On September 11, 2001, terrorists attacked the United States of America, hoping to cause us a major economic setback. However, one of the defining factors of the American people is our resilience.

In the aftermath of 9/11, some entrepreneurs decided to expand, refusing to allow external circumstances to control their outcomes. Examples of these entrepreneurs included the likes of Nick Woodman of GoPro (2002); Martin Eberhard and Marc Tarpenning founded Tesla (2003), with Elon Musk joining in 2004; and even Mark Zuckerberg, who began working on Facebook in 2003, launching it in 2004. Along with well-known entrepreneurs, there are thousands of lesser-known stories of entrepreneurs who chose to launch their ventures during that uncertain time in history. I was one of them, launching my first entrepreneurial success in 2002.

These entrepreneurs, in light of external forces telling them otherwise, had the **self-efficacy** to believe it could be done and could figure it out. Despite the turmoil of the times, they were **optimistic** about the possibilities and **imagined** what the various outcomes could be. They **prospected** the best and worst-case scenarios, along with the future possibilities. They didn't allow over-optimism to cloud the importance of prospecting. Finally, they **acted courageously** at a time when most played it safe and then **owned all their outcomes** along the way.

Speaking for myself, as an entrepreneur for over two decades now, I did not do any of this perfectly. There were times I blamed others or circumstances. Sometimes I was the pessimistic CEO who viewed some unfortunate events as permanent. Other times, I ignored the worst-case scenarios and failed at effective prospection, and there were moments I sat with my ideas too long and failed to act courageously. Of course, I have also fallen prey to believing opinions about me expressed from total strangers. Despite my imperfections, the previous seven laws—from EntreClarity to Entre-Vigor—addressed these moments where I lacked the recognition of agency. The first seven laws helped me get over the bumps and bruises I encountered along the way. They enabled me to continue down the exciting and wild path of entrepreneurship.

We end with EntreAgency because, as I said at the beginning of this chapter, it is the keystone of EntreThrive. It gives the other laws the freedom to move and work effectively in our lives as entrepreneurs. In turn, the other laws provide the right environment for our agency to work more effectively within each of us.

More than any law before it, EntreAgency bridges the gap between what lies between us and the Good Life, as it's truly all the laws wrapped into one continuous act of free will.

Next Actions

- Evaluate your EntreAgency by reviewing a recent setback you experienced and identify what explanatory style you used to deal with it, optimistic or pessimistic.

- Take our *EntreAgency Assessment* to identify areas of strength and improvement when it comes to your own personal agency. Go to **EntreThrive.com/Resources** to download this exercise.

The Science Behind the Law of EntreAgency and How It Can Help You to Create Your Good Life

Agency is the psychological state that is the main precursor to the massive growth and change we experience throughout civilization. Seligman's current research on agency highlights how psychological forces of self-efficacy, optimism, and innovation (defined as agency) preempt civilization's massive upheaval that occurred from monumental innovations.[14] Contrary to beliefs whereby the new innovations changed the way humans think and behave, agency has been the lever that catapulted the growth of our civilization. By engaging in habits and practices that support one's agency, entrepreneurs can drive change and achieve positive outcomes in their life, thereby leading to greater happiness.

Self-efficacy, which is closely related to resilience, can drive entrepreneurs towards their goals by *proactively* taking steps to mold their future.[15]

Optimism is an essential factor that contributes to positive outcomes and life satisfaction. Research highlights the importance of cultivating an optimistic outlook as it can help entrepreneurs reach their intended goals. Martin Seligman's book, *Learned Optimism,* indicates that learning how to develop a positive explanatory style can help entrepreneurs focus on their strengths and reframe negative thoughts.[16]

Conclusion: Traci's Story

E xercising our agency is not often easy, especially in moments of crisis. On September 3, 2020, our good friends, David and Traci Parker were in a head-on motorcycle accident while on their way to Yellowstone National Park for a brief getaway. David lost his life that evening, while Traci was miraculously spared but left with a severely damaged leg. David and Traci are the parents of five children, with their two youngest still at home (aged 11 and 8 at the time of Dave's death). Our entire community mourned the tremendous loss of this incredible human being. My birthday was the day before Dave's death and I still cherish the happy belated birthday message he sent, just a few hours before his passing.

Dave founded and operated a thriving insurance business, Parker Insurance, with the largest portfolio of individual policies in the state. Dave was the entrepreneurs' insurance agent and one of the most respected, kind-hearted, and personable individuals I had the honor of knowing. Always engaging, present, and willing to take the shirt off his back for anyone in need. Though Dave had a team to support him, including Traci, his clients demanded his attention because he was "their guy." Always available and rarely unable to step in and help.

So, you can only imagine what his passing meant to Parker Insurance. In Traci's mind, it was really Dave Parker Insurance.

If you're familiar with the private insurance world, policy renewals happen in a six-week window, beginning November 1st and ending December 15th, just two months after Dave's death. This is the busy-busy season for all healthcare insurance agents. In light of this looming deadline, let's take a quick moment to list just a few of the incredibly difficult circumstances Traci now had to navigate.

- The unexpected and crushing loss of her loving husband and best friend.

- Being a support to five grieving kids, including her two little ones still at home, who needed her more than ever.

- Planning and attending Dave's funeral, in light of her own critical injuries.

- Recovering for several weeks in the hospital and almost losing her foot. (The healing process was extensive as Traci had multiple surgeries and could not walk on her own for nearly a year after the accident).

- COVID-19 was in full effect, with the hospital limiting who could visit her.

- Taking care of customers and team members (with November 1st approaching) without years of experience in doing so. She was involved in the business previously, but as internal support.

- Most importantly, the uncertainty of how she was going to pull it all off and take care of her family! This alone would have been almost too much to handle.

My bullet points really don't give her circumstances the proper justice, but what would you do in this situation? After sitting down with Traci and getting a deeper perspective into what she was truly dealing with at the time, I asked this same question of myself. How would I have responded? I will tell you what Traci did. She made the conscious choice to move forward. She found a deep and abiding why, early on, that illuminated her way as she was surrounded by darkness on all sides.

My purpose in interviewing Traci was to incorporate her story into the law of EntreFaith, which certainly was the case for her. She told me she would not have made it through if she had not exercised tremendous faith. However, after listening to her, it dawned on me that all eight laws seem to have manifested themselves throughout her journey in the following ways:

1. EntreClarity—Her why illuminated her way through a storm of challenges. Her why is sacred and personal but helps bring clarity when things grow dark.

2. EntreCreate—Traci and her team had to create a better way to fill the gap Dave's passing left. They have constantly created new and better ways of doing business.

3. EntreGrit—Her staying power was fueled by her calling to create positive opportunities for the Parker team and to inspire others to exercise their faith. This calling has also spilled over into her personal life as well.

4. EntreConnections—Traci leaned on the right people she knew would guide her to where she needed to go.

5. EntreFaith—She knew her future was more promising than what she could see or feel, by trusting in herself, others, and God to get her through many uncertainties. Traci's faith in all these areas has inspired an entire community.

6. EntreHabits—The simple habit of getting out of bed each morning and doing the little things elevated her performance personally and professionally.

7. EntreVigor—Traci's positive energy is contagious because she consistently tames the wild Mustang Mind. Her mind and body are aligned.

8. EntreAgency—Traci's self-efficacy, optimism, and imagination unleashed her free will to act in a positive, healthy way, when it could have been easy for her to give up on herself, allow pessimism to overtake her mind, and squash her imagination by blaming others for her circumstances. She chose to not let her circumstances define her and her future. She chose to frame the past in a way that opened up limitless possibilities.

Shortly after Dave's death, her brother Brian stepped up in a major way and moved his family to Idaho, became a licensed agent, and helped Traci get through those tough few months. He and Traci would visit clients, even in her wheelchair, so customers knew the business was still open and capable of taking care of their needs. With the help of Brian, and the entire Parker team, Traci has led Parker Insurance to unprecedented growth in the last three years.

Traci's journey to creating the Good Life for herself is ongoing. Some days she is still overwhelmed with grief by the loss of Dave but she would be the first one to tell you that she is also happy. She is living her best life. Because she has chosen to do so. Unknowingly, she has implemented these eight laws better than I probably ever will and at an accelerated speed.

Creating the Good Life for yourself does not mean you are creating a life free of worry, heartache, physical ailments, grief, and uncertainties. It is about creating a life that flourishes, regardless of circumstances. It's about learning how to respond to what life gives you, irrespective of challenges that you may not have even brought on yourself, as was the case for Traci. Let this be the goal for all of us! To lean into these eight laws, so you can accelerate financial freedom and create the Good Life for yourself.

In summary, these eight laws have been my guide through some rather difficult challenges as an entrepreneur.

I am grateful for each one of them in the following ways:

Clarity on my why, my Guiding Truths help me align my breakaways with what I really want in this life.

Taking time to **Create** enables me to dream of the life and freedom I desire.

My calling to help entrepreneurs flourish has fortified my **Grit**.

Being congruent, present, and engaged with my deepest **Connections** brings me joy.

My **Faith** allows me to trust myself, others, and God to make the impossible possible.

My positive unconscious **Habits** fortify my key character strengths and help me progress on others.

My **Vigor** is a result of learning to tame my Mustang Mind, creating mind and body alignment.

Self-efficacy, optimism, imagination, and prospection grant me the **Agency** to choose a positive past, present, and future.

As stated in the introduction, the Good Life is a mindset because life as an entrepreneur is often unpredictable, thrilling, challenging, and fun. We can't expect a smooth ride, most of the time! It is up to us to create the Good Life irrespective of our circumstances. No one will do it for us. We must choose it. Once we do, we realize our entrepreneurial journey can bring us joy, opportunities, and freedom at every turn. This is my hope for you, and those you love, as you incorporate these eight laws.

I have enjoyed being your guide throughout this book. For more guidance, connection, and resources that can help you deepen your journey towards the Good Life, please visit **EntreThr ive.com/Resources** to download free tools, research resources, enroll in our courses and programs, and become a member of our EntreThrive community of entrepreneurs.

For home care (elderly care in the home) entrepreneurs or executives, check out our Breakaway Accelerator programs designed to help home-care providers **think** bigger, **keep** their A players, accelerate their growth, **transform** their agency, and create **freedoms** in your life you never before thought were possible. To learn more and apply for one of our upcoming *Breakaway Immersives,* go to **BreakawayAccelerator.com.**

Notes

1. Robert Waldinger and Marc Schulz, *The Good Life: Lessons from the World's Longest Scientific Study of Happiness,* (New York: Simon & Schuster, 2023), 3.

2. Claude Fernet, Oliver Torrès, Stéphanie Austin, and Josée St-Pierre, "The psychological costs of owning and managing an SME: Linking job stressors, occupational loneliness, entrepreneurial orientation, and burnout," *ScienceDirect.com,* accessed April 2023, https://www.sciencedirect.com/science/article/pii/S221305861530 0097 .

3. Dennis Jacobe, "Work Is Labor of Love for Small-Business Owners," *Gallup.com,* August 23, 2005, https://news.gallup.com/poll/18088/work-labor-love-smallbu siness-owners.aspx .

4. Amina Omrane, Amal Kammoun, and Claire Seaman, "Entrepreneurial Burnout: Causes, Consequences and Way Out," *FIIB Business Review* 7, no. 1, (2018): 28-42, https://doi.org/10.1177/2319714518767805 .

5. Claude Fernet et al.

6. Omrane et al.

7. Sabine Bährer-Kohler, ed., *Burnout for Experts: Prevention in the Context of Living and Working,* 13th ed. (New York: Springer, 2013).

8. Ute Stephan, "Entrepreneurs' Mental Health and Well-Being: A Review and Research Agenda," *Academy of Management Perspectives* 32, no. 3 (2018): 290–322, https://doi.org/10.5465/amp.2017.0001 .

9. Xueyan Wei, Shuangxin Cang, and Robert D. Hisrich, "Entrepreneurial Stressors as Predictors of Entrepreneurial Burnout," *Psychological Reports* 116, no. 1 (2015): 74-88, https://doi.org/10.2466/01.14.PR0.116k13w1 .

10. Martin Luther King, Jr., " If you can't fly then run," *Goodreads.com,* accessed June 2023, https://www.goodreads.com/quotes/26963-if-you-can-t-fly-then-ru n-if-you-can-t-run .

11. Nadav Shir and Carol Ryff, "Entrepreneurship, Self-Organization, and Eudaimonic Well-Being: A Dynamic Approach," *Entrepreneurship Theory and Practice* 46, no. 6 (2021), https://doi.org/10.1177/10422587211013798 .

12. Shir and Ryff.

13. Barbara L. Fredrickson, *Positivity: Top-Notch Research Reveals the 3-to-1 Ratio That Will Change Your Life*, (New York: Harmony, 2009).

14. Elizabeth Perry, "The Path to Self-Acceptance, Paved Through Daily Practice," *BetterUp.com* (blog), August 5, 2021, https://www.betterup.com/blog/self-acceptance .

15. Dan Sullivan and Dr. Benjamin Hardy, *The Gap and the Gain: The High Achiever's Guide to Happiness, Confidence, and Success* (Carlsbad, CA: Hay House Business, 2021).

16. Sullivan and Hardy.

17. Perry.

18. Perry.

19. Ed Mylett, "Matthew McConaughey Himself Said This Was His Best Interview!," April 18, 2023, YouTube video, 0:01 to 5:00, https://www.youtube.com/watch?v=MP16l2gQjqg .

20. Mylett.

21. Lawrence R. Samuel, "For a Happy Thanksgiving, Add 'Flow' to Family, Friends, Food, and Football," *Psychology Today*, November 23, 2021, https://www.psychologytoday.com/us/blog/psychology-yesterday/202111/happy-thanksgiving-add-flow-family-friends-food-and-football .

22. Richard M. Ryan and Edward L. Deci, "Self-Determination Theory and the Facilitation of Intrinsic Motivation, Social Development, and Well-Being," *American Psychologist* 55, no. 1 (2000): 68-78, https://selfdeterminationtheory.org/SDT/documents/2000_RyanDeci_SDT.pdf .

23. Jim Carrey, "I Think Everybody Should Get Rich and Famous So They Can See That That's Not the Answer," *Quote Investigator*, accessed May 2023, https://quoteinvestigator.com/2022/11/09/rich-famous/ .

24. Gabriele Oettingen, Hyeon-ju Pak, and Karoline Schnetter, "Self-Regulation of Goal-Setting: Turning Free Fantasies About the Future Into Binding Goals," *Journal of Personality and Social Psychology* 80, no. 5 (2001): 736-753, https://psycn et.apa.org/doi/10.1037/0022-3514.80.5.736 .

25. Gabriele Oettingen, *Rethinking Positive Thinking: Inside the New Science of Motivation* (London: Current, 2015).

26. Kendra Cherry, "11 Characteristics of Self-Actualized People," *Very Well Mind*, February 22, 2023, https://www.verywellmind.com/characteristics-of-self-actual ized-people-2795963 .

27. Henri Tajfel, "The Achievement of Inter-Group differentiation" in *Differentiation between Social Groups: Studies in the Social Psychology of Intergroup Relations,* ed. H. Tajfel (London: Academic Press, 1978), 7 7-100; Henri Tajfel and J. C. Turner, "An Integrative Theory of Intergroup Conflict" in *The Social Psychology of Intergroup Relations,* eds. William G. Austin and Stephen Worchel (Monterey, CA: Brooks/Cole, 1979), 33-47.

28. Rami M. Shapiro, "The stories we tell about ourselves," in "Quotes about the stories we tell ourselves," Quote Stats, accessed May 2023, https://quotestats.co m/topic/quotes-about-the-stories-we-tell-ourselves/ .

29. Jim Collins, "Turning Goals Into Results: The Power of Catalytic Mechanisms," *Harvard Business Review,* July-August 1999, https://hbr.org/1999/07/turning-g oals-into-results-the-power-of-catalytic-mechanisms .

30. Melissa Madeson, "Seligman's PERMA+ Model Explained: A Theory of Wellbeing," *PositivePsychology.com*, February 24, 2017, https://positivepsychology.com/ perma-model/#achievements .

31. Vince Lombardi, "Most people fail not because of lack of desire," in "35 Inspirational Quotes on Commitment," ed. Asad Meah, *Awakenthegreatnesswithin.com,* updated May 2023, https://www.awakenthegreatnesswithin.com/35-inspiration al-quotes-on-commitment/ .

32. Martin E. P. Seligman, "PERMA and the Building Blocks of Well-Being," The Journal of Positive Psychology 13, no.4 (2018): 333-335, https://doi.org/10.108 0/17439760.2018.1437466.

33. Edward L. Deci and Richard M. Ryan, "The 'What' and 'Why' of Goal Pursuits: Human Needs and the Self-Determination of Behavior," *Psychological Inquiry*, 11, no. 4 (2000): 227-268, https://doi.org/10.1207/S15327965PLI1104_01.

34. Carl A. Benware and Edward L. Deci, "Quality of Learning with an Active versus Passive Motivational Set," *American Educational Research Journal*, 21, no. 4 (Winter 1984): 755-765, https://doi.org/10.3102/00028312021004755; Edward L. Deci, A. J. Schwartz, L. Sheinman, and Richard M. Ryan, "An Instrument to Assess Adults' Orientations Toward Control versus Autonomy With Children: Reflections on Intrinsic Motivation and Perceived Competence," *Journal of Educational Psychology* 73, no. 5 (1981): 642–650, https://doi.org/10.1037/0022-0 663.73.5.642; Wendy S. Grolnick and Richard M. Ryan, "Autonomy Support in Education: Creating the Facilitating Environment" in *New Directions in Educational Psychology* (Oxfordshire, UK: Routledge, 1987), ebook 9780203993019.

35. M. F. Steger, P. Frazier, S. Oishi, and M. Kaler, "The Meaning in Life Questionnaire: Assessing the Presence of and Search for Meaning in Life," *Journal of Counseling Psychology* 53, no. 1 (2006): 80-93, https://doi.org/10.1037/0022-01 67.53.1.80.

36. Eric S. Kim, Jennifer K Sun, Nansook Park, and Christopher Peterson, "Purpose in Life and Reduced Incidence of Stroke in Older Adults: 'The Health and Retirement Study,'" *Journal of Psychosomatic Research* 74, no. 5 (2013): 427-432, https://doi.org/10.1016/j.jpsychores.2013.01.013.

37. Neal Krause, "Evaluating the Stress-Buffering Function of Meaning of Life Among Older People," *Journal of Aging and Health* 19, no. 5 (2007): 792-812, https://doi.org/10.1177/0898264307304390.

38. Ed Diener and Martin E. P. Seligman, "Very Happy People," *Psychological Science* 13, no. 1 (2002): 81-84, https://doi.org/10.1111/1467-9280.00415.

39. Mihayli Csikszentmihalyi, *Flow: The Psychology of Optimal Experience*, (New York: Harper & Row, 1990).

40. Nicola S. Schutte and John M. Malouff, "Connections Between Curiosity, Flow and Creativity," *Sciencedirect.com*, January 2020, https://www.sciencedirect.com /science/article/abs/pii/S0191886919304878 .

41. Anthony D. Fredericks, "Why Curiosity Is Necessary for Creativity," *Psychology today.com*, February 11, 2022, https://www.psychologytoday.com/us/blog/creative-insights/202202/why-curiosity-is-necessary-creativity .

42. VIA Institute on Character, "The 24 Character Strengths," accessed April 2023, https://www.viacharacter.org/character-strengths .

43. VIA Institute on Character.

44. VIA Institute on Character.

45. Eaton Business School, "Here's Why Creativity Is so Crucial for Entrepreneurship?" accessed April 2023, https://ebsedu.org/blog/why-creativity-is-crucial-for-entrepreneurship/ .

46. Molly St. Louis, "5 Entrepreneurs That Are Shaking Up Education," Inc.com, July 25, 2017, accessed April 2023, https://www.inc.com/molly-reynolds/5-entrepreneurs-that-are-shaking-up-education.html.

47. Gabriele Oettingen, Hyeon-ju Pak, and Karoline Schnetter, "Self-Regulation of Goal-Setting: Turning Free Fantasies About the Future Into Binding Goals," Journal of Personality and Social Psychology 80, no. 5 (2001): 736-753, https://doi.org/10.1037/0022-3514.80.5.736.

48. Lisa Capretto, "How James Taylor Jump-Starts His Creative Process," Huffpost.com, November 25, 2015, https://www.huffpost.com/entry/james-taylor-creative-process_n_5654b961e4b0879a5b0cb9e5.

49. Tyler DeVries, summary of "Creativity: The Psychology of Discovery and Invention," Tylerdevries.com, accessed April 2023, https://tylerdevries.com/book-summaries/creativity/.

50. Mihaly Csikszentmihalyi, *Creativity: Flow and the Psychology of Discovery and Invention* (New York: Harper Collins, 2009).

51. Csikszentmihalyi.

52. Csikszentmihalyi.

53. Eckhart Tolle Quotes, AZquotes.com, accessed April 2023, https://www.azquotes.com/quote/535440 .

228

54. Linda Naiman. "The Surprising Connection Between Gratitude and Creativity," *CreativityatWork.com*, accessed April 2023, https://www.creativityatwork.com/what-is-the-connection-between-creativity-and-gratitude/ .

55. John J. Miller, Ken Fletcher, and Jon Kabat-Zinn, "Three-Year Follow-Up and Clinical Implications of a Mindfulness Meditation-Based Stress Reduction Intervention in the Treatment of Anxiety Disorders," *General Hospital Psychiatry* 17 (1995): 192-200, https://doi.org/10.1016/0163-8343(95)00025-m.

56. Charalampos Mainemelis and Dionysios D. Dionysiou, "Play, Flow, and Timelessness," in *The Oxford Handbook of Creativity, Innovation, and Entrepreneurship*, (July 9, 2015): 121-140, https://doi.org/10.1093/oxfordhb/9780199927678.013.0006.

57. Mihaly Csikszentmihalyi, "Creativity: Flow and the Psychology of Discovery and Invention," accessed April 2023, http://www.mkc.ac.in/pdf/study-material/psychology/2ndSem/UNIT-4-flow-and-creativty-AG.pdf.

58. Csikszentmihalyi.

59. Angela Duckworth, Grit: The Power of Passion and Perseverance, (New York: Scribner, 2016).

60. Duckworth.

61. James Clear, "How Successful People Practice Better, Not More," *Businessinside r.com*, August 17, 2013, accessed March 2023, https://www.businessinsider.com/how-successful-people-practice-2013-8 .

62. Colin O'Brady, "The Impossible Row," ColinO'Brady.com, accessed March 2023, https://www.colinobrady.com/theimpossiblerow.

63. Discovery, "Training for the Drake," Facebook.com, December 10, 2019, accessed March 2023, https://www.facebook.com/watch/?v=850381442069528.

64. Duckworth.

65. Duckworth.

66. Duckworth.

67. Eva de Mol, Violet T. Ho, and Jeffrey M. Pollack, "Predicting Entrepreneurial Burnout in a Moderated Mediated Model of Job Fit," *Journal of Small Business Management*, 56, no. 3 (2018): 392-411, https://doi.org/10.1111/jsbm.12275 .

68. Jie Li, Mengyuan Fang, Wangshuai Wang, Gong Sun, and Zhiming Cheng, "The Influence of Grit on Life Satisfaction: Self-Esteem as a Mediator," *Psychologica Belgica* 58, no. 1 (2018): 51-66, https://psychologicabelgica.com/articles/10.533 4/pb.400 .

69. Duckworth.

70. Martin Seligman, "PERMA and the Building Blocks of Well-Being," *The Journal of Positive Psychology* 13, no. 4, (2018): 333-335, https://doi.org/10.1080/17439 760.2018.1437466.

71. Kamlesh Singh and Shalini Duggal Jha, "Positive and Negative Affect, and Grit as Predictors of Happiness and Life Satisfaction," *Journal of the Indian Academy of Applied Psychology* 34, no. 2 (2008): 40-45, https://www.researchgate.net/publication/285749956_Positive_and_ne gative_affect_and_grit_as_predictors_of_happiness_and_life_satisfaction.

72. M. R. Leary and R. F. Baumeister, "The Need to Belong: Desire for interpersonal attachments as a fundamental human motivation," *Psychological Bulletin* 117, no. 3, (1995): 497-529, https://psycnet.apa.org/doi/10.1037/0033-2909.117.3.497 .

73. Isaac Prilleltensky and Olga Prilleltensky, *How People Matter: Why It Affects Health, Happiness,Love, Work and Society* (Cambridge: Cambridge University Press, 2021).

74. Kathryn Armstrong and Bernd Debusmann, Jr., "US Surgeon General Vivek Murthy recounts bout of profound loneliness," *BBCNews,* https://www.bbc.co m/news/world-us-canada-65461723 .

75. Robert Waldinger and Marc Schulz, M. *The Good Life: Lessons from the World's Longest Scientific Study of Happiness.* (New York: Simon and Schuster, 2023).

76. Waldinger and Schulz.

77. Kim Klyver, Benson Honig, and Paul Steffens, "Social Support Timing and Persistence in Nascent Entrepreneurship: Exploring When Instrumental and Emotional Support Is Most Effective," *Small Business Economics* 51, no. 3 (December 6, 2017): 709-734, https://doi.org/10.1007/s11187-017-9964-5 .

78. Kim Klyver, Benson Honig, and Paul Steffens, "Social Support Timing and Persistence in Nascent Entrepreneurship: Exploring When Instrumental and Emotional Support Is Most Effective," *Small Business Economics* 51, no. 3 (December 6, 2017): 709- 734, https://doi.org/10.1007/s11187-017-9964-5 .

79. Shelly L. Gable and Harry T. Reis, "Good News! Capitalizing on Positive Events in an Interpersonal Context," in *Advances in Experimental Social Psychology* 42, ed. Mark P. Zanna, (San Diego, CA: Academic Press, 2010): 195-257, https://psycn et.apa.org/doi/10.1016/S0065-2601(10)42004-3 .

80. Jan Inge Jenssen and Harry F. Koenig, "The Effect of Social Networks on Resource Access and Business Start-Ups," *European Planning Studies* 10, no. 8 (2010): 1039-1046, https://doi.org/https://doi.org/10.1080/0965431022000031301 .

81. David Stanley, "Congruent Leadership: Values in Action," *Journal of Nursing Management* 16, no. 5 (July 2008): 519-524, https://doi.org/https://doi.org/10.1111/j.1365-2834.2008.00895.x .

82. Ruilin Huang, "Regain Control of Time in Remote Work: Incorporating the 'Self' and the 'Home,' Proceedings, *Academy of Management,* July 24, 2023, https://doi.org/10.5465/AMPROC.2023.12424abstract .

83. C. A. Bulger, R. A. Matthews, and M. E. Hoffman, "Work and personal life boundary management: Boundary strength, work/personal life balance, and the segmentation-integration continuum," *Journal of Occupational Health Psychology*, 12(4), 365.

84. I. J. Jonsdottir and K. Fridriksdottir, "Active listening: Is it the forgotten dimension in managerial communication?" *International Journal of Listening*, 34(3), 178-188.

85. Jessica Gilsoul, Vincent Libertiaux, and Fabienne Collette, "Cognitive fatigue in young, middle-aged, and older: Breaks as a way to recover," *Applied Psychology*, 71(4), 1565–1597, https://doi.org/10.1111/apps.12358 .

86. P. Sedlmeier, J. Eberth, M. Schwarz, D. Zimmermann, F. Haarig, S. Jaeger, and S. Kunze, "The psychological effects of meditation: A meta-analysis," *Psychological Bulletin*, 138(6), 1139–1171, https://doi.org/10.1037/a0028168.

87. Justin Harmon and Lauren Duffy, "Turn off to tune in: Digital disconnection, digital consciousness, and meaningful leisure," *Journal of Leisure Research*, 54:5, 539-559, DOI: 10.1080/00222216.2023.2220699.

88. A. M. Grant and F. Gino, "A little thanks goes a long way: Explaining why gratitude expressions motivate prosocial behavior," Journal of Personality and Social Psychology, 98(6), 946.

89. Faith Ozbay, Douglas C. Johnson, Eleni Dimoulas, C. A. Morgan III, Dennis Charney, and Steven Southwick, "Social Support and Resilience to Stress," *Psychiatry* 4, no.5 (2007): 35-40, https://www.ncbi.nlm.nih.gov/pmc/articles/PMC 2921311/.

90. John Paul Stephens, Emily Heaphy, and Jane E. Dutton, "High Quality Connections," in *The Oxford Handbook of Positive Organizational Scholarship*, eds. Kim S. Cameron and Gretchen M. Spreitzer, Oxford Library of Psychology (2011; online edition, Oxford Academic, 21 Nov. 2012), accessed November 20, 2023, https://doi.org/10.1093/oxfordhb/9780199734610.002.0004.

91. Stephens, Heaphy, and Dutton.

92. Roy F. Baumeister, "Need to Belong Theory," in *Handbook of Theories of Social Psychology*, eds. Paul A. M. Van Lange, Arie W. Kruglanski, and E. Tory Higgins (Thousand Oaks, CA: Sage, 2012): 121-140, https://doi.org/10.4135/97814462 49215.

93. James J. Lynch, *The Broken Heart: The Medical Consequences of Loneliness* (New York: Basic Books, 1979).

94. Ed Diener and Martin E. P. Seligman, "Very Happy People," *Psychological Science* 13, no. 1 (2002): 81-84, https://doi.org/10.1111/1467-9280.00415.

95. Karen J. Reivich and Martin E. P. Seligman, "Master Resilience Training in the U.S. Army," *American Psychologist* 66, no. 1 (2011): 25-34, https://doi.org/10.1 037/a0021897.

96. Isaac Prilleltensky and Olga Prilleltensky, *How People Matter: Why It Affects Health, Happiness, Love, Work and Society*, (Cambridge: Cambridge University Press, 2021).

97. "President Uchtdorf: 'Come, Join with Us,'" TheChurchNews.com, October 4, 2 0 1 3 , https://www.thechurchnews.com/2013/10/5/23223962/president-uchtdorf-co me-join-with-us#:~:text=%22Faith%20is%20to%20hope%20for,the%20people%2 0in%20the%20Church.

98. Martin Luther King, Jr., "Faith is taking the first step even when you do not see the whole staircase," in *I love Motivational Quotes (blog)*, accessed June 2023, https://i-love-motivational-quotes.org/author/martin-luther-king-jr .

99. Henry Cloud, *Necessary Endings: The Employees, Businesses, and Relationships That All of Us Have to Give Up in Order to Move Forward* (New York: Harper Business, 2011).

100. Courtney E. Ackerman, "What is Self-Efficacy Theory?" *Positivepsychology.com*, updated April 26, 2023, https://positivepsychology.com/self-efficacy/ .

101. Cloud.

102. Deltav, "The Big Lie About Trust—5 Reasons Why Trust Is Not Earned," *Peak Solutions* (blog), May 30, 2015, https://www.peaksol.com/blog/the-big-lie-abou t-trust-5-reasons-why-trust-is-not-earned/ .

103. Mike Robbins, "Trust is Granted, Not Earned," *Mike-Robbins.com* (blog), March 5, 2021, https://mike-robbins.com/trust-is-granted-not-earned/ .

104. Mahatma Ghandi, "I believe in trusting," *Goodreads.com*, accessed May 2023, https://www.goodreads.com/quotes/357449-i-believe-in-trusting-trust-begets-tr ust-suspicion-is-foetid#:~:text=Sign%20Up%20Now-,I%20believe%20in%20trust ing.,yet%20lost%20in%20the%20world.

105. Jim Collins, "First Who, Then What," *JimCollins.com*, accessed May 2023, https://www.jimcollins.com/concepts/first-who-then-what.html#:~:text=First%2 0Who%2C%20Then%20What%E2%80%94get,where%20to%20drive%20the%20 bus.

106. Steven M. R. Covey, David Kasperson, McKinlee Covey, and Gary T. Judd, *Trust and Inspire: How Truly Great Leaders Unleash Greatness in Others*, reprint ed. (New York: Simon & Schuster, 2023).

107. Jeff Whittle, "Right People—Right Seats," *EOSWorldwide.com* (blog), accessed May 2023, https://www.eosworldwide.com/blog/106234-eos-right-people-right-seats?utm_term=&utm_medium=ppc&utm_campaign=Dynamic+Brand&utm_source=ad words&hsa_net=adwords&hsa_ad=652314645782&hsa_mt=&hsa_acc=306657 8213&hsa_src=g&hsa_tgt=dsa-1991173513145&hsa_grp=151035902767&hsa_cam=19879578382&hsa_kw=&hsa_ver=3&gclid=Cj0KCQjwhfipBhCqARIsA H9msblxd8AaDZtYiuQcF7XUvS_gwnasX6KRyhxeYOQPdhMzP8H84lwejw8 aAmeNEALw_wcB.

108. E. R. Mackenzie, D. E. Rajagopal, M. Meilbohm, and R. Lavizzo-Mourey, "Spiritual Support and Psychological Well Being: Older Adults' Perceptions of the Religion and Health Connection," *Alternative Therapies in Health and Medicine* 6, no. 6 (November 2000): 37-45, https://pubmed.ncbi.nlm.nih.gov/11076445/.

109. Sandra King Kauanui, Kevin D. Thomas, Arthur Rubens, and Cynthia L. Sherman, "Entrepreneurship and Spirituality: A Comparative Analysis of Entrepreneurs' Motivation," *Journal of Small Business and Entrepreneurship* 23, no. 4 (2010): 621-635, https://doi.org/10.1080/08276331.2010.10593505.

110. James Dennis LoRusso, *Spirituality, Corporate Culture, and American Business: The Neoliberal Ethic and the Spirit of Global Capital*, of *Critiquing Religions: Discourse, Culture, Power*, series ed. Craig Martin (London: Bloomsbury Academic, 2017).

111. Kauanui et al.

112. Lindsey Williams, "Watch: BYU Speeches Shares the Parable of the Bicycle in This New Inspiring Short," *LDSLiving.com* (March 4, 2021), accessed May 2023, https://www.ldsliving.com/watch-byu-speeches-shares-the-parable-of-the-bicycle-in-this-new-inspiring-short/s/94025.

113. David B. Yaden, Johannes C. Eichstaedt, Margaret L. Kern, Laura K. Smith, Anneke Buffone, David J. Stillwell, Michal Kosinski, Lyle H. Ungar, Martin E. P. Seligman, and Andrew H. Schwartz, "The Language of Religious Affiliation: Social, Emotional, and Cognitive Differences," *Social Psychological and Personality Science* 9, no. 4 (2018): 444-452, https://doi.org/10.1177/1948550617711228.

114. Christopher Peterson and Martin E. P. Seligman, *Character Strengths and Virtues: A Handbook and Classification* (Oxford: American Psychological Foundation/Oxford University Press, 2004).

115. David B. Yaden, Cassondra L. Batz-Barbarich, Vincent Ng, Hoda Vaziri, Jessica N. Gladstone, James O. Pawelski, and Louis Tay, "A Meta-Analysis of Religion/Spirituality and Life Satisfaction," *Journal of Happiness Studies* 23, no. 8 (December 2022): 4147-4163, https://doi.org/10.1007/s10902-022-00558-7.

116. John F. Helliwell and Shun Wang, "Trust and Well-Being," *National Bureau of Economic Research*, W15911, (revised 2011), https://doi.org/10.3386/w15911.

117. Yaden, Eisenstaedt, Kern et al.

118. "Mission: Impossible - Dead Reckoning Part One | Tom Cruise | The Biggest Stunt in Cinema History," *YouTube*, uploaded by IMAX, December 19, 2022, https://www.youtube.com/watch?v=WLtpQpKY7fw&t=2s .

119. Ibid.

120. Wendy Wood, *Good Habits, Bad Habits: The Science of Making Positive Habits Stick*, illus. ed. (New York: Farrar, Straus, and Giroux, 2019): 24.

121. James Clear, *Atomic Habits: An Easy and Proven Way to Build Good Habits and Break Bad Ones*, (New York: Avery, 2018).

122. Emily Pronin, "The Introspection Illusion," in *Advances in Experimental Psychology* 41, ed. Mark P. Zanna (2009): 1-67, https://doi.org/10.1016/S0065-2601(08)00401-2 .

123. Wood.

124. Wood, 28.

125. VIA Institute on Character, "The 24 Character Strengths," accessed April 2023, https://www.viacharacter.org/character-strengths .

126. VIA Institute on Character.

127. Ryan Niemiec, *Character Strengths Interventions: A Field Guide for Practitioners* (Boston: Hogrefe Publishing, 2017).

128. Wood.

129. Clear.

130. Thomas L. Webb and Paschal Sheeran, "Identifying Good Opportunities to Act: Implementation Intentions and Cue Discrimination," *European Journal of Social Psychology* 34, no. 3 (2004): 407-419, https://doi.org/10.1002/ejsp.205 .

131. Wood.

132. Wood.

133. Wood.

134. VIA Institute on Character, "Self-Regulation," accessed May 2023, https://www.viacharacter.org/character-strengths/self-regulation .

135. Courtney E. Ackerman, "What Is Self-Regulation? (+95 Skills and Strategies)," *PositivePsychology.com*, accessed May 2023, https://positivepsychology.com/self-regulation/#why-self-regulation .

136. Tayyab Rashid and Afroze Anjum, "340 Ways to Use VIA Character Strengths," https://tayyabrashid.com/pdf/via_strengths.pdf .

137. Richard M. Ryan and Edward L. Deci, "Self-Determination Theory and the Facilitation of Intrinsic Motivation, Social Development, and Well-Being," *American Psychologist* 55, no. 1 (2000): 68-78, https://doi.org/10.1037/0003-066X.55.1.68 .

138. Niemiec.

139. Ryan and Deci.

140. Wendy Wood and David T. Neal, "Healthy Through Habit: Interventions for Initiating and Maintaining Health Behavior Change," *Behavioral Science & Policy* 2, no. 1 (2016): 89-93, https://behavioralpolicy.org/publications/past-issues/.

141. "Mustengo," *Wordsense Online Dictionary*, accessed May 2023, https://www.wordsense.eu/mestengo/ .

142. Tony Robbins, "My teacher Jim Rohn taught me a simple principle: every day, stand guard at the door of your mind," *Quotefancy.com*, accessed May 2023, https://quotefancy.com/quote/923128/Tony-Robbins-My-teacher-Jim-Rohn-taught-me-a-simple-principle-every-day-stand-guard-at .

143. James Allen, *As a Man Thinketh* (New York: TarcherPerigee, 2008).

144. "Wild Horse Wild Ride," uploaded by Popcornflix, February 11, 2016, https://www.youtube.com/watch?v=RX28swUzD-U .

145. Suzanne Bennett, "Tips for Training Mustangs and Wild Horses," *HorsesandFo als.com (blog)*, April 22, 2023, https://horsesandfoals.com/training-mustangs-wi ld-horses/.

146. John Medina, *Brain Rules*, second ed. (Seattle: Pear Press, 2014).

147. Medina.

148. Gabriella Rosen Kellerman and Martin E. P. Seligman, *Tomorrowmind: Thriving at Work—Now and in an Uncertain Future* (New York: Simon & Schuster, 2023).

149. Albert Ellis, "The Revised ABC's of Rational-Emotive Therapy (RET)," *Journal Rational-Emotive Cognitive-Behavior Therapy* 9 (1991): 139-172, https://doi.org /10.1007/BF01061227 .

150. Chris Crowley and Dr. Henry S. Lodge, *Younger Next Year: Live Strong, Sexy, Fit, and Smart—Until You're 80 and Beyond* (New York: Workman Publishing Company, 2019).

151. "Cycling — The Exercise for Positive Mental Health," *MensLine Australia*, accessed May 2023, https://mensline.org.au/mens-mental-health/cycling-the-exercise-for-positive-me ntal-health/#:~:text=It%20improves%20creative%20thinking%3A%20The,both% 20physical%20and%20mental%20function .

152. Dr. Joe Dispenza, *Breaking the Habit of Being Yourself: How to Lose Your Mind and Create a New One* (Carlsbad, CA: Hay House Inc., 2013).

153. Dispenza.

154. "Synchronize," *Dictionary.com*, accessed May 2023, https://www.dictionary.co m/browse/synchronization .

155. Catherine Moore, "What Is Eudaimonia? Aristotle and Eudaimonic Wellbeing," *PositivePsychology.com*, updated September 6, 2023, accessed April 2023, https:/ /positivepsychology.com/eudaimonia/ .

156. Lord Byron, "There Is Pleasure in the Pathless Woods," *poemAnalysis.com*, accessed April 2023, https://poemanalysis.com/lord-byron/there-is-pleasure-in-the-pathl ess-woods/ .

157. Alison Pritchard, Miles Richardson, David Sheffield, and Kirsten McEwan, "The Relationship Between Nature Connectedness & Eudaimonic Well-Being: A Meta-Analysis," *Journal of Happiness Studies* (April 2019), https://link.springer. com/article/10.1007/s10902-019-00118-6 .

158. John Lubbock, "Rest is not idleness," *Brainyquote.com*, accessed May 2023, https://www.brainyquote.com/quotes/john_lubbock_107976#:~:text=John%20 Lubbock%20Quotes&text=Rest%20is%20not%20idleness%2C%20and%20to%2 0lie%20sometimes%20on%20the,means%20a%20waste%20of%20time.

159. Kathryn E. Schertz and Marc G. Berman, "Understanding Nature and Its Cognitive Benefits," *Current Directions in Psychological Science* 28, no. 5 (2019): 496-502, https://doi.org/10.1177/09637214198541 .

160. Windy Dryden, Daniel David, and Albert Ellis, "Rational Emotive Behavior Therapy," in *Handbook of Cognitive Behaviors,* ed. Keith S. Dobson, third ed. (New York: Guilford Press, 2010): 226-276, (https://nibmehub.com/opac-service/pdf/read/Handbook%20of%20Cognitive-Behavioral%20Therapies.pdf#page=241).

161. Peter Schulman, "Applying learned optimism to increase sales productivity," *Journal of Personal Selling and Sales Management* 19, no. 1, (1999): 31-37, https://d oi.org/10.1080/08853134.1999.10754157.

162. Surjeet Singh and Nov Rattan Sharma, "Self-regulation as a Correlate of Psychological Well-Being," *Indian Journal of Health and Wellbeing* 9, no. 3, (2018): 441-444, https://www.i-scholar.in/index.php/ijhw/article/view/181481.

163. Martin E. P. Seligman, "Agency in Greco-Roman Philosophy," *The Journal of Positive Psychology*, 16, no. 1 (2021): 1-10. https://doi.org/10.1080/17439760.20 20.1832250 .

164. Seligman.

165. Seligman.

166. Albert Bandura, "Self-Efficacy: The Foundation of Agency," in *Control of Human Behavior, Mental Processes, and Consciousness: Essays in Honor of the 60th Birthday of August Flammer*, eds. Walter J. Perrig and Alexander Grob (Mahwah, NJ: Lawrence Erlbaum Associates, 2000), 16-31.

167. Martin E. P. Seligman, *Learned Optimism: How to Change Your Mind and Your Life*, reprint ed. (New York: Vintage, 2006), 96.

168. Seligman.

169. Seligman.

170. Seligman.

171. Albert Einstein, "Imagination is everything," *Brainyquote*, accessed June 2023, https://www.brainyquote.com/quotes/albert_einstein_384440 .

172. Gabriella Rosen Kellerman and Martin E. P. Seligman, *Tomorrowmind: Thriving at Work—Now and in an Uncertain Future* (New York: Simon & Schuster, 2023).

173. Victor Hugo, "No army can withstand the strength of an idea," *Goodreads.com*, accessed June 2023, https://www.goodreads.com/quotes/2302-no-army-can-wit hstand-the-strength-of-an-idea-whose .

174. Pat Summitt, "Responsibility equals accountability equals ownership," *Quotefancy*, accessed June 2023, https://quotefancy.com/quote/1552190/Pat-Summitt-R esponsibility-equals-accountability-equals-ownership-And-a-sense-of .

175. Jocko Willink and Leif Babin, *Extreme Ownership: How U.S. Navy SEALs Lead and Win* (New York: St. Martin's Press, 2017).

176. Seligman, "Agency in Greco-Roman philosophy," 1-10.

177. Ralf Schwarzer and Lisa Marie Warner, "Perceived self-efficacy and its relationship to resilience,"in *Resilience in Children, Adolescents, and Adults: Translating Research into Practice, The Springer Series on Human Exceptionality*, eds. Sandra Prince-Embury and Donald H. Saklofske, 12 (New York: Springer Business Science Media, 2012): 139-150.

178. Seligman, *Learned Optimism*.

Acknowledgments

To my family: As noted in the opening dedication, I have an exceptional family who have supported me throughout this journey called life. I am eternally grateful for them, particularly my beautiful and courageous wife Heather.

To Igniting Souls and Ethos Collective Publishing: Grateful to Kary Oberbrunner and the entire Igniting Souls team for believing in me, providing next-level support, and getting behind my "Opus."

To Mike Koenigs and his team. Deeply thankful for your honest mentorship, guiding me on a powerful journey to creating my "next act," and opening up my mind to limitless possibilities.

To Dr. Martin Seligman, my former professor and the father of positive psychology, whose groundbreaking work provided the inspiration I needed to write this book.

To my extraordinary classmates, faculty, and team, led by James Pawelski and Leona Brandwene, at the University of Pennsylvania's Master of Applied Positive Psychology (MAPP) program. This book would not have been possible without all of you.

To Paula Toledo, my fellow and gracious MAPP classmate, for your tireless dedication, ensuring that the science of well-being, Positive Psychology, was expertly interwoven throughout this work and for your continued guidance.

To my daughters and team members, Brinley and Anna. To Brinley for lending her exceptional gifts as my personal advisor, editor, writer, and design manager. To Anna for having the courage to learn and expand her talents in digital marketing and beyond.

To my exceptional strategic assistant, Megan, who I confidently and thankfully gave trust to from day one. Her amazing ability to open up space so I could create was instrumental in finishing this work. Also, a special shout out to Lana, my former strategic assistant of many years, who supported me through several crazy ideas and ventures.

To Dan Sullivan and his one-of-a-kind entrepreneurial coaching program, Strategic Coach®. This program has helped me become a more well-rounded and successful entrepreneur, husband, and father and has empowered me to strive to 10x my life. Grateful for the many friendships of bigger thinking entrepreneurs I have gained from my association with Coach. Special thanks to my coaches over the years including Dan Sullivan, Lee Brower, Chad Johnson, and Adrienne Duffy.

To the many entrepreneurial mentors in my life who believed in me, mentored me, invested in my ventures, and sacrificed their time to guide me along the way. A special acknowledgment to a few mentors in particular: Steve Everhart and Shane Argyle, who believed in a young twenty-eight-year-old entrepreneur. I will forever be grateful. Then, later on in my entrepreneurial journey, Erik Madsen, Dale Green (in Memoriam), Todd Austin, and Chris Bennett. All of them demonstrated great faith in me, which in turn elevated my faith in myself, others, and in God.

To EOS Worldwide®, founded by Gino Wickman, that provided the exceptional business model my 10x company needed in 2016, giving me the space to flourish personally and begin my journey towards positive psychology and entrepreneurial well-being.

Finally, to the renowned development expert, Brian Tracy, who inspired me twenty-two years ago to change my mindset and create my dreams as an entrepreneur. His endorsement of this book, all these years later, is extremely humbling and is a reminder to keep striving to achieve your biggest goals and desires.

About the Author

Over the span of more than twenty years, Aaron has founded and scaled award-winning multi-million-dollar companies that have positively impacted the lives of thousands throughout North America. Aaron has received numerous awards recognizing his leadership, vision, and service. He has been a sought-after national speaker since 2006 and enjoys empowering his audiences to make positive changes in their personal and professional lives.

Aaron began his entrepreneurial journey in healthcare. In his second start-up, his visionary leadership changed the trajectory of the home-care Industry when he founded the Best of Home Care® award program and created an innovative benchmarking and performance platform, which has positively impacted the lives of thousands of entrepreneurs and the millions of seniors under their care.

He received a Master in Applied Positive Psychology from the University of Pennsylvania, where he studied under renowned psychologists and well-being experts, including Dr. Martin Seligman, the founder of Positive Psychology. This life-changing program helped Aaron discover his personal path to flourishing. Now, as an executive leadership coach, Aaron works to help other entrepreneurs eliminate unhealthy stress and find their personal path to flourishing.

Aaron's passions lie in road cycling (completing LoToJa, a two hundred-mile one-day bike race four times) and fly-fishing. He's been married to his lovely wife Heather since 1996, and they are the proud parents of six beautiful children.

The Law of **EntreClarity**™

Your Guiding Truths
Illuminate Your Way

Discover your path to success with the
EntreClarity Guide—a powerful tool designed
to ignite self-discovery and unleash your
potential through your Guiding Truths and
future Breakaways!

Visit **EntreThrive.com/guidingtruths** to begin!

In-Home Care Breakaway Accelerator Immersive

5 BREAKAWAY SECRETS

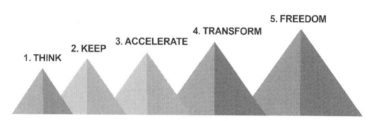

1. THINK
2. KEEP
3. ACCELERATE
4. TRANSFORM
5. FREEDOM

COMMUNITY

During this immersive experience, you will learn and quickly apply the skills needed to:

- **Think** bigger
- **Keep** the right people in your circle
- **Accelerate** the growth of your company
- **Transform** your personal and professional life
- Experience **freedoms** you never thought possible

Join Aaron Marcum for our next Breakaway Accelerator Immersive by applying at **breakawayaccelerator.com**.

Join our **In-Home Care Breakaway Community**

An exclusive free community for in-home care founders who want to **stop living the lie of the either/or.** You can thrive personally and professionally! Gain access to free tools, engaging courses, and opportunities to connect with other in-home care founders and entrepreneurs who are creating The Good Life for themselves.

Visit **breakawayaccelerator.com/community**

Join our Homecare Breakaway Community Today!

CONNECT WITH AARON

Follow him on your favorite
social media platform today

ENTRETHRIVE.COM

For in-home care founders and executives go to:
Breakawayaccelerator.com

THIS BOOK IS PROTECTED INTELLECTUAL PROPERTY

The author of this book values Intellectual Property. The book you just read is protected by Easy IP™, a proprietary process, which integrates blockchain technology giving Intellectual Property "Global Protection." By creating a "Time-Stamped" smart contract that can never be tampered with or changed, we establish "First Use" that tracks back to the author.

Easy IP™ functions much like a Pre-Patent™ since it provides an immutable "First Use" of the Intellectual Property. This is achieved through our proprietary process of leveraging blockchain technology and smart contracts. As a result, proving "First Use" is simple through a global and verifiable smart contract. By protecting intellectual property with blockchain technology and smart contracts, we establish a "First to File" event.

Powered By Easy IP™

LEARN MORE AT EASYIP.TODAY